Performance Appraisals: Strategies for Success

Performance Appraisals:
Strategies for Success

Diane Arthur

 American Management Association®

© 2008 American Management Association. All rights reserved.

This material may not be reproduced, stored in a retrieval system, or transmitted in whole or in part, in any form or by any means, electronic, mechanical, photocopying, recording, or otherwise, without the prior written permission of the publisher.

ISBN-13: 978-0-7612-1462-5
ISBN-10: 0-7612-1462-3

Printed in the United States of America.

10 9 8 7 6 5 4 3 2 1

Contents

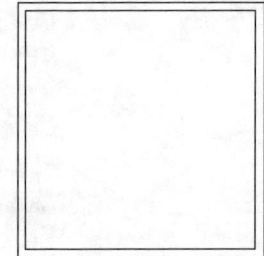

About This Course

The performance appraisal process is a critical tool for achieving organizational success, but there are few tasks managers dislike more. *Performance Appraisals: Strategies for Success* gives managers the knowledge, skills, and awareness to approach this process with confidence and enthusiasm. By providing practical, hands-on information and real-world scenarios, this course gives managers the tools to understand and apply every aspect of the performance appraisal process: reviewing employees' past performance; assessing their success in meeting previously set objectives, helping them set new, achievable objectives; and pursuing a career development plan.

Assessments, diagrams, checklists, and exercises help students gain a thorough understanding of the performance appraisal process and the manager's responsibilities with regard to coaching and counseling and establishing and adhering to standards of performance. Step-by-step instructions help students prepare for the critical face-to-face meeting with employees and complete the written review. Special topics in performance appraisal are addressed, including the principles of workplace motivation, understanding what workers really want, the role of mentoring programs, performance appraisals for remote employees, the merits of managerial feedback, and the advantages and disadvantages of Web-based performance appraisals.

Diane Arthur is the president of Arthur Associates Management Consultants, Ltd., a human resources development firm based in Northport, New York. She has more than twenty-five years of HR experience as a consultant, course developer, and workshop leader, covering all facets of HR, including legal issues, the employment process, testing, compensation, performance management, training and development, and employee relations.

She has written many books for AMACOM, including *The Employee Recruitment and Retention Handbook*, four editions of *Recruiting, Interviewing, Selecting & Orienting New Employees*, *The Complete Human Resources Writing Guide*, two editions of *Managing Human Resources in Small and Mid-Sized Companies*, and *Workplace Testing: An Employer's Guide to Policies and Practices*.

Her Self-Study programs for the American Management Association include *Fundamentals of Human Resources Management; Successful Interviewing: Techniques for Hiring, Coaching, and Performance Management Meetings;* and *Success through Assertiveness.* In addition, Diane Arthur has written numerous HR articles for publications such as IBM's *Beyond Computing, Human Resource Executive, HR Reporter,* and *The Wall Street Journal.* She is listed in the 26th Edition of *Who's Who in the East* and appears on the American Management Association's Wall of Fame.

How to Take This Course

This course consists of text material for you to read and three types of activities (the pre- and post-test, in-text exercises, and end-of-chapter review questions) for you to complete. These activities are designed to reinforce the concepts introduced in the text portion of the course and to enable you to evaluate your progress.

PRE- AND POST-TESTS

Both a pre-test and post-test are included in this course. Take the pre-test before you study any of the course material to determine your existing knowledge on the subject matter. Submit one of the scannable answer forms enclosed with this course for grading. On return of the graded pre-test, complete the course material. Take the post-test after you have completed all the course material. By comparing results of the pre-test and the post-test, you can measure how effective the course has been for you.

To have your pre-test and post-test graded, please mail your answer forms to:

Educational Services
American Management Association
P.O. Box 133
Florida, NY 10921

All tests are reviewed thoroughly by our instructors and will be returned to you promptly.

THE TEXT

The most important component of this course is the text, where the concepts and methods are presented. Reading each chapter twice will increase the likelihood of your understanding the text fully.

We recommend that you work on this course in a systematic way. Reading the text and working through the exercises at a regular and steady pace will help ensure that you get the most out of this course and retain what you have learned.

In your first reading, concentrate on getting an overview of the chapter content. Read the learning objectives at the beginning of the chapter first. They will act as guidelines to the major topics of the chapter and identify the skills you should master as you study the text. As you read the chapter, pay attention to the headings and subheadings. Find the general theme of each section and see how that theme relates to others. Don't let yourself get bogged down with details during the first reading; simply concentrate on understanding and remembering the major themes.

In your second reading, look for the details that underlie the themes. Read the entire chapter carefully and methodically, underlining key points, working out the details of examples, and making marginal notes as you go. Complete the activities.

ACTIVITIES

Interspersed with the text of each chapter you will find a series of activities. These can take a variety of forms, including essays, short-answer quizzes, or charts and questionnaires. Completing the activities will enable you to try out new ideas, practice and improve new skills, and test your understanding of the course content.

THE REVIEW QUESTIONS

After reading a chapter and before going to the next chapter, work through the Review Questions. Answering the questions and comparing your answers to those given will help you grasp the major ideas of that chapter. If you perform these self-check exercises, you will develop a framework in which to place material presented in later chapters.

GRADING POLICY

The American Management Association will continue to grade examinations and tests for one year after the course's out-of-print date.

If you have questions regarding the tests, the grading, or the course itself, call Educational Services at 1-800-225-3215 or send an e-mail to ed_svc@amanet.org.

Pre-Test

Performance Appraisals: Strategies for Success

Course Code 95083

Instructions: Record your answers on one of the scannable forms enclosed. Please follow the directions on the form <u>carefully</u>. Be sure to keep a copy of the completed answer form for your records. <u>No photocopies will be graded.</u> When completed, mail your answer form to:

**Educational Services
American Management Association
P.O. Box 133
Florida, NY 10921**

1. At the end of the appraisal meeting, the manager should work together with the employee in setting new goals. This process should include:
   (a) the promise of a raise if the employee meets his or her new goals.
   (b) a timeline to review progress and identify problems.
   (c) configured and prefigured tasks.
   (d) written progress reports.

2. The appraisal method that involves the greatest amount of input from numerous sources, and may be considered the one most likely to provide a well-rounded evaluation is called:
   (a) a behaviorally anchored rating scale.
   (b) a graphic rating scale
   (c) management by objectives.
   (d) a 360-degree evaluation.

Do you have questions? Comments? Need clarification?
Call Educational Services at 1-800-225-3215, ext. 600,
or email at ed_svcs@amanet.org.

3. Managers need to balance the amount of talking they do with listening. In reality, managers should devote no more than:
   (a) twenty-five percent of the time talking.
   (b) fifteen percent of the time talking.
   (c) an equal amount of time talking and listening.
   (d) the amount of time required by the employee—some employees are better listeners than talkers.

4. An important step in the preparation stage is for managers to anticipate possible employee reactions to their appraisals. One way of dealing with an overconfident employee is to:
   (a) emphasize the areas in which they need to improve.
   (b) provide them with additional, challenging responsibilities.
   (c) ask them to present documentation as evidence of all their accomplishments.
   (d) mirror their behavior.

5. An effective performance appraisal system requires the cooperation and input of human resources practitioners, managers, and employees in which everyone involved in the process is responsible for:
   (a) ensuring consistency between comments, ratings, and any recommended action to be taken.
   (b) completing a self-evaluation.
   (c) applying applicable employment laws.
   (d) looking for ways in which to enhance or improve the performance appraisal system.

6. Web-based performance appraisals are gaining acceptance in some organizations because they:
   (a) are cost-effective.
   (b) eliminate the need for managers to sit, face-to-face, with an employee and deal with possible adverse reactions.
   (c) make it easier for managers to comply with review-related responsibilities.
   (d) allow managers to give every employee the same basic review, thereby eliminating any possible charges of discrimination.

7. An important question managers should ask themselves during the preparation stage of conducting employee performance appraisals is:
   (a) Does the employee respect me and trust that I will give him or her a fair appraisal?
   (b) Have I objectively measured the employee's work record against the requirements of the job?
   (c) Do I have a right to appraise an employee performing a job that I, myself, have never held?
   (d) Would I be better off asking a professional to write the review? Then I can just refer to it during the face-to-face meeting.

8. The first of four key ways in which employees can benefit from and use performance appraisals that have nothing to do with money is:
  (a) the opportunity to receive a clearer understanding of what they are expected to do.
  (b) the opportunity to let human resources know what really goes on in their department.
  (c) nothing—this is a trick question; everything has to do with money.
  (d) the opportunity to justify an out-of-town conference to learn new skills.

9. Of the seven motivational theories described, the one that stands out as contrary to all the others is:
  (a) Theory Z.
  (b) the Hierarchy of Needs Theory.
  (c) the Theory of Acquired Needs.
  (d) Theory X.

10. You will discuss four main areas in a performance appraisal meeting: past performance, previously set performance objectives, new performance objectives, and:
  (a) the employee's career development plan.
  (b) the percentage raise being recommended.
  (c) how the employee plans to work on areas requiring improvement.
  (d) how the employee can benefit from the company's mentor program.

11. One of the best-known pieces of civil rights legislation and the most widely used, in that it protects several classes of people and pertains to so many employment situations, including performance appraisals, is the:
  (a) Civil Rights Act of 1991.
  (b) Civil Rights Act of 1964.
  (c) Immigration Reform and Control Act of 1986.
  (d) Equal Pay Act of 1963.

12. Many managers resist participating in the performance appraisal process because:
  (a) they are not getting paid enough money to deal with the range of possible employee reactions to their reviews.
  (b) they have never been taught how.
  (c) employees should conduct self-appraisals.
  (d) performance appraisals belong in the hands of human resources.

13. Of the five recommended interviewing questions, the type that allows for the evaluation of reasoning abilities, thought processes, attitudes, creativity, work style, and one's approach to different tasks is:
    (a) probing.
    (b) open-ended.
    (c) hypothetical.
    (d) competency-based.

14. The type of coaching that requires managers to be attentive and attuned to each employee's individual work habits, routines, and current assignments is called:
    (a) spontaneous coaching.
    (b) planned coaching.
    (c) directive coaching.
    (d) nondirective coaching.

15. Throughout the year, between formal performance appraisal reviews, managers are responsible for observing and noting:
    (a) employee accomplishments and areas requiring improvement.
    (b) documented evidence to support termination.
    (c) initiative.
    (d) how successful employees are at meeting performance objectives from the previous year.

16. As part of a progressive disciplinary procedure, following a second written warning for excessive absenteeism, an employee should be:
    (a) terminated.
    (b) suspended with or without pay.
    (c) sent for counseling.
    (d) issued a third written warning.

17. Managers are advised to begin planning the contents of a written performance appraisal approximately:
    (a) one month prior to the due date.
    (b) one week prior to the due date.
    (c) two weeks prior to the due date.
    (d) two months prior to the due date.

18. The primary distinction between coaching and counseling is that coaching involves day-to-day interaction between managers and employees in which managers regularly offer assistance, support, praise, and constructive criticism. Counseling, on the other hand, involves:
    (a) progressive discipline.
    (b) legal counsel.
    (c) the final stage before termination.
    (d) a structured interaction between managers and their employees; managers focus on particular work-related issues.

19. In order to be effective, a performance appraisal system should practical, workable, and viewed by all as:
    (a) a matter of law.
    (b) disposable; that is, replaced as soon as a new appraisal is written.
    (c) a helpful tool for achieving organizational goals.
    (d) nonnegotiable.

20. Managers commonly have an aversion to conducting negative appraisal meetings. They hope that the employee's work will improve on its own, or that:
    (a) the employee will take pity on them and shape up.
    (b) the employee will transfer or terminate.
    (c) the employee will seek counseling.
    (d) human resources will realize what is going on and step in to intervene.

21. When writing job descriptions, prior experience requirements should accurately and realistically reflect the level and nature of the position. An example of a tangible experience requirement is:
    (a) a pleasant personality.
    (b) a proven ability to successfully communicate with attendees of training programs.
    (c) a college degree.
    (d) a demonstrated ability to lift cartons weighing 20–40 lbs.

22. Mentoring relationships are determined on the basis of:
    (a) the defined needs of the mentees and the interests of the mentors.
    (b) the status of the mentor in the organization.
    (c) how much help the mentee requires.
    (d) a lottery.

23. Subjective language reflects one's personal opinion and may be subject to interpretation. An example is that:
    (a) Jill has the technical skills required of this job.
    (b) Jill has five years' previous experience performing similar tasks.
    (c) Jill has demonstrated her ability to do this job.
    (d) I think Jill has what it takes to do this job!

24. When evaluating the long-term effectiveness of communication skills, managers find measurable results are more likely to continue when they provide:
    (a) annual increases in pay.
    (b) constructive criticism and training.
    (c) ongoing feedback and encouragement.
    (d) promotional and transfer opportunities.

25. Managerial feedback can serve to:
   (a) identify areas requiring improvement.
   (b) maximize a manager's ability to fairly and accurately appraise workers.
   (c) reveal a side of a manager no one has ever seen before.
   (d) determine whether he or she has executive potential.

The Performance Appraisal Process: An Overview

focus

Learning Objectives

By the end of this chapter, you should be able to:

- Identify the objectives of a performance appraisal process.
- Explain managerial resistance to participating in the performance appraisal process.
- Describe a common misconception about performance appraisals.
- Recognize the many benefits and uses of performance appraisals for human resources (HR) practitioners, managers, and the organization as a whole.
- Articulate the elements of an effective performance appraisal system.
- Differentiate among the respective performance appraisal responsibilities of managers, human resources practitioners, and employees.
- Recognize obstacles to achieving performance objectives.

Many years ago when I worked in the human resources department of a bank, the senior vice president to whom I reported called me in to his office. It was nearly 5:00PM on a Friday afternoon, and I was anxious to leave. He assured me that what he had to say would only take a few minutes. Then he added, "You're going to want to hear this." "That sounds ominous," I commented. He laughed and replied, "Not at all; I think you'll be pleased."

He sat down behind his extra-large desk and I took a seat in the nearest chair across from him. I noted that he had a piece of paper in front of him, but because of the width of his desk, I could not discern what it was. "As you well know," he began, "every employee receives an annual performance appraisal. Today it's your turn. I'm going to go through each category on the form; then, when I'm done, you can comment, if you like." He looked down at the form in front of him and proceeded to address each category, identifying in broad terms how he viewed my work. He spoke for about five minutes, never looking up; when he reached the final category he leaned back with a smile and remarked, "Pretty good, huh?"

It was hard to disagree with his overall praise for my work; yet, I felt somewhat cheated. He had not commented on any specific achievements, or acknowledged the positive feedback I had received from several department heads in the past several months. I also wanted to talk about my goals for the coming year. My thoughts were interrupted when he said, "Well, I guess that's it. Let's both get our weekend started!" I was so taken aback, all I could think to say was, "Don't you want me to sign the review?" He laughed and said, "Why would you want to sign this? There's nothing written on it—it's just a blank performance appraisal form; I was just using it as a guide!"

He held up what had until then been blocked from my view: it was, indeed, a blank form. His final comment was the most unnerving to me: "Listen, since we're in HR we get to tell all the other departments to turn in appraisals, but we don't have to do them. We know that they don't really mean anything!"

Nothing could have been further from the truth. If he had bothered to review the objectives of the performance appraisal process, he would have appreciated the many benefits and multiple uses of employee reviews. Furthermore, he would have been compelled to acknowledge the merits of an effective appraisal system and accepted his role and areas of responsibility in the process.

OBJECTIVES OF THE PERFORMANCE APPRAISAL PROCESS

The primary objective of a performance appraisal program is to ensure the maximum utilization of every employee's skills, knowledge, and interests. (Since some organizations use the term "performance appraisal" and others use "performance review," the two phrases will be used interchangeably throughout this course.) This results in a more motivated workforce, which, in turn, positively impacts productivity and increases an organization's competitive edge. In addition, employer-employee relations are enhanced, resulting in less strife for managers.

How can any one program accomplish so much? The answer lies in how performance appraisals are viewed; that is, as being beneficial to employees, appraisers, and the organization as a whole. Too often, unsatisfactory results stem from managerial resistance to conducting appraisal meetings or completing accompanying forms, viewing the process as time-consuming, difficult, or nonproductive. Employees may also approach the process negatively, seeing it as simply faultfinding and a way for organizations to justify holding back raises. And management often overlooks the fact that the degree of effectiveness and commitment on the part of their human resources largely determines the success of an organization.

A poorly planned or subjectively implemented system, or the absence of an appraisal system altogether can greatly weaken an organization and, ultimately, its ability to perform. On the other hand, tapping into the needs of both managers and staff will greatly improve its chances of success.

Effective performance appraisal systems go beyond their primary objective of ensuring the maximum utilization of every employee's skills, knowledge, and interests. They also serve to enhance *employer-employee relations, HR development*, and *employee career development.*

Additional *employer-employee relations* objectives include:

- Strengthening the overall working relationship between managers and employees
- Developing a mutual understanding between managers and employees with regard to performance expectations, goals, and measurement criteria
- Encouraging employees to openly express themselves with regard to performance-related issues
- Encouraging managers to examine their own strengths and areas requiring improvement
- Helping managers effectively coach and counsel their employees

Additional *HR development objectives* include:

- Allowing for more productive uses of an organization's human resources
- Identifying "mismatches" in hiring
- Providing supportive data for decisions concerning salary increases, transfers, promotions, demotions, and disciplinary action up to and including termination
- Identifying specific ways to expand beyond the existing talent pool of an organization by clearly understanding the skills of its current human resources
- Identifying an organization's top employees for future human resource planning purposes

Additional *employee career development objectives* include:

- Providing feedback on past performance according to established standards of performance and specific job responsibilities
- Planning developmental opportunities by identifying employee strengths and areas requiring improvement
- Helping evaluate an individual's potential
- Motivating employees to both establish and achieve personal goals that are compatible with organizational goals

 **Think About It...**

Concerning your organization's current performance appraisal system . . .

What is its primary objective?

_____

_____

Overall, how successful is your organization in meeting its primary objective?
Extremely Successful _____ Somewhat Successful _____ Not At All Successful _____

If your organization's primary performance objective is not to "ensure the maximum utilization of every employee's skills, knowledge, and interests," how receptive would it be to adjusting its focus?
Very Receptive _____ Somewhat Receptive _____ Not At All Receptive _____

What are some additional objectives of your organization's appraisal system?

_____

_____

_____

How successful is your organization in meeting these secondary objectives?
Extremely Successful _____ Somewhat Successful _____ Not At All Successful _____

If your organization does not currently have a formal performance appraisal system . . .
How receptive would it be to establishing one and adopting "the maximum utilization of every employee's skills, knowledge, and interests" as its primary objective?
Extremely Receptive _____ Somewhat Receptive _____ Not At All Receptive _____

Performance objectives can best be accomplished when the organization, its managers, and employees all work together while recognizing that, despite specific goal variations, everyone is working toward achieving some measure of success. Identifying common denominators that link the different definitions of success for all concerned is what determines a successful performance appraisal program.

OBSTACLES TO ACHIEVING PERFORMANCE OBJECTIVES

It is critical that everyone concerned be aware of two key obstacles that can easily interfere with the achievement of primary and secondary performance objectives: lack of clarity and lack of mutual respect.

Lack of Clarity

We all get caught up in the details of our work and bogged down with one crisis after another, to the point where we often lose sight of the big picture. A cloud of minutia can distort our ability to focus on key objectives, resulting in our inability to work together toward common goals. This lack of clarity can impact every aspect of the workplace including performance systems. Unfortunately, many organizations view appraisals as an annual event. Accordingly, they tend to ignore performance-related issues when they occur, choosing instead to address them after the fact during a yearly review.

To maintain a clear focus and sense of direction, every manager should follow these three steps:

- *Step 1*: Review long- and short-term departmental, organizational, and individual employee goals
- *Step 2*: Assess the relationship and degree of compatibility among departmental, organizational, and individual employee goals
- *Step 3*: Identify areas of incompatibility and determine ways in which they can be more closely aligned

The frequency of following these three steps will depend largely on the size of an organization, the complexity of its objectives, whether it is in a start-up or established mode, and the degree and level of independence at which departments and separate geographic locations function. At a minimum, managers should go through these steps quarterly; for decentralized work environments with multi-tiered objectives, addressing them on a monthly basis would be more prudent.

Before beginning this exercise, you may want to make several photocopies to be used for additional goals.

✎ Exercise: Three Steps to Achieving Greater Clarity

Step 1:

Select one specific short- or long-term organizational goal and one departmental goal. Be specific:

Organizational Goal:

_____

_____

Departmental Goal:

_____

Now select one employee from your department and identify a work-related goal that he or she has shared with you. If this has not happened, select one of your own work-related goals:

Employee Goal:

_____

_____

Step 2:

Assess the relationship and degree of compatibility between the three goals you have identified. Rate them as being:
Extremely Compatible _____ Somewhat Compatible _____
Not At All Compatible _____

Step 3:

If you did not check off "Extremely Compatible," identify one specific area of incompatibility. For example, your departmental goal might be to increase the number of sales by 30% within the next six months. This is in line with the organization's goal for increased growth and production. However, your top sales representative has indicated that her personal goal is to scale back on customer contact and focus, instead, on working toward moving into a supervisory position.

Area of Incompatibility:

_____

_____

_____

Now identify possible ways in which the goals that are incompatible can be more closely aligned:

Desired Result: _____

People Involved: _____

Resources Needed: _____

Impediments: _____

Possible Ramifications: _____

Projected Time Frame: _____

Repeat these steps for each area of incompatibility. Revisit them on a regular basis to achieve greater clarity and assess progress made.

Lack of Mutual Respect

On March 15, 2005, Naomi Churchill Earp, vice chair of the U.S. Equal Employment Opportunity Commission (EEOC), spoke at the Society for Human Resource Management's 22nd Annual Employment Law and Legislative Conference. Prior to describing some of the cases being heard by the EEOC, Ms. Earp stated the need for greater respect in the workplace;

specifically, for managers to respect workers as well as workers to respect their managers.

Many HR professionals also suggest that respect, along with recognition and organizational commitment, are critical components of effective employee performance. Unfortunately, many people think of respect as being directed upward; that is, toward someone in a position higher than one's own. In the workplace, that means managers respect members of senior management, and employees respect their managers, as well as members of senior management. This certainly makes sense and contributes to an efficient work environment. Unfortunately, it is one-directional, and as such, is more likely to foster performance-related issues.

To be truly effective, respect has to flow in multiple directions (Exhibit 1–1). Employees need to respect managers as well as members of senior management; managers need to respect members of senior management and employees; and members of senior management need to respect managers and employees. In addition, everyone needs to respect their colleagues and anyone else involved in the achievement of their organizational, departmental, or personal goals, such as consultants and vendors, customers, clients, and guests. Finally, self-respect is essential. Without multi-directional respect, the achievement of primary and secondary performance objectives will be compromised.

Respect takes time to cultivate. As with any relationship, people in an office need time to become comfortable with one another's styles and habits. It is easy to disregard or disrespect someone because of a single error, comment, or look, thus damaging what could have been a relationship of mutual respect. Managers are quick to want to fire employees for simple transgressions; employees may form opinions of those in management based solely on rumors.

 **xhibit 1–1**
Mutual Respect

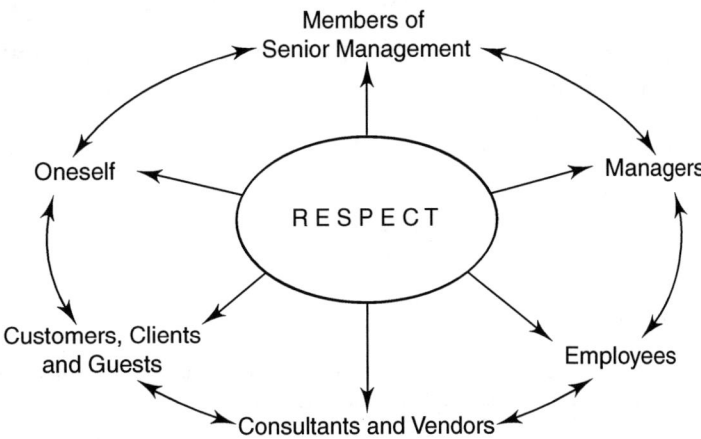

 **Think About It...**

Think of an individual in your office who, upon first meeting, you did not particularly like, but then later learned to respect. The person can be someone who reports to you, a manager, a member of senior management to whom you report, or a colleague. In the space provided, describe your initial impression of this person (names are not necessary):

When I first met this person I thought he/she was

_____

_____

The reason I felt this way was because

_____

_____

At what point did you start to feel differently toward this person?

_____

_____

Why do you think you started to feel differently?

_____

_____

Describe how your relationship has changed now that you respect this person.

_____

_____

MANAGERIAL RESISTANCE TO PARTICIPATING IN THE PERFORMANCE APPRAISAL PROCESS

It probably comes as no surprise to learn that there are many managers who view performance appraisals as a burden. Specific reasons commonly cited include:

- Conducting performance appraisals should not be part of a manager's job; it belongs in the hands of human resources.
- It is uncomfortable telling employees that their work is anything less than outstanding, even when their performance is sub par.
- Employees already know how they are doing and should not need to be told in a formal setting once a year.
- Poor performers are just going to continue doing what they did before the performance appraisal, so there is really no point in going through the motions.
- Employees are only concerned with how much money they are going to receive.

Let's examine each of these objections:

1. *Performance appraisals belong in the hands of human resources.* In all fairness, it is not uncommon for people to be hired or promoted into a position without being told the full scope of their responsibilities. When it comes to managers, the "pieces" that are missing often involve aspects of employer-employee relations, including discipline or evaluation. It is also understandable for managers to assume performance appraisals fall under the purview of human resources. After all, what could be more HR-related than employee evaluations?

   The key to resisting this area of accountability is for managers to view performance appraisals as an opportunity as opposed to a chore. This is a chance to learn about how employees feel about their jobs, the department in which they work, and the organization as a whole. In addition, managers can learn how employees feel they can best contribute to organizational goals while achieving personal aspirations.

   Managers are advised to work with HR in determining how to complete the appraisal form and conduct the meeting in the most effective manner.

2. *Telling employees that their work is sub par.* Imagine making this statement to an employee during a performance appraisal meeting: "Cheryl, I like you, I really do; you tell great jokes and you're not a bad dresser. But your work performance is really awful. You don't follow instructions, people complain about you behind your back, and if you would just quit it would be better for everyone in the department."

   Aside from violating every employer-employee relations rule ever written, this speech will have Cheryl either looking at you with sad eyes that will make you feel like a villain, or looking at you so angrily that you will want to hire a bodyguard to accompany you home! But the fact is, lying to someone whose work is below required standards does not help them, you, their colleagues, or the organization. The key to communicating unpleasant information is to focus on the facts without personalizing the situation or succumbing to emotion. This topic will be expanded upon in Chapter 6.

3. *Employees do not need to be told how they are doing.* Everyone needs feedback regardless of how well they are doing, top performers still need to have their work acknowledged, and poor performers need guidelines for improvement. In addition, every employee deserves the opportunity to discuss interests and aspirations. Managers can then consider how employee goals mesh with organizational objectives.

4. *Poor performers will never change.* Managers who essentially ignore their employees throughout the year and then begrudgingly sit down with them for a few minutes annually because HR tells them they must are undoubtedly going to have poor performers who will never change. This will occur either because the poor performers are not motivated to change or they do not know that aspects of their work are unacceptable. By communicating about issues when they occur, it is far more likely that managers will be able to summarize past performance during the appraisal meeting and

then move ahead to discuss methods for continued improvement and future goals.

5. *Employees are only concerned with money.* Most motivational experts agree that money is not a prime motivator; they suggest that employees are often more motivated by factors such as being able to make a contribution to the organization, having their work acknowledged, and being rewarded in numerous non-monetary ways.

One of the times money is categorized as a prime motivator is when an employee learns that a colleague performing similar or less significant tasks earns more. Money then comes to represent inequity.

✎ Exercise: Managerial Resistance to Participating in the Performance Appraisal Process

Consider the following scenario: Jake was promoted to a managerial position eight months ago. He knows that he has to conduct performance appraisals for each of the four employees reporting to him, and has worked with HR in determining how to complete the appraisal form and conduct the meeting in an effective manner. Still, he feels uncomfortable with regard to one particular employee named Rose. He "inherited" Rose from his predecessor, Mark, who warned Jake about her surly attitude and spotty attendance. Mark had admittedly never spoken to Rose about her behavior, since he knew he was retiring soon. Now it's up to Jake.

In this scenario, how should Jake prepare for his meeting with Rose?

_____

_____

How should Jake expect Rose to react to criticism of her work for the first time?

_____

_____

_____

Would Jake be better off leaving matters as they are, not mentioning Rose's attitude or attendance? _____ yes _____ no

Explain your answer.

_____

_____

_____

HINTS, SUGGESTIONS, AND SOME ANSWERS

In preparing for his meeting with Rose, Jake should:

• Talk with Mark concerning specific incidences during which Rose demonstrated a "surly attitude."

• Talk with those with whom Rose has had regular contact to determine if others viewed her as having a "surly attitude."

- Review Rose's attendance record to determine what Mark defined as "spotty."
- Obtain guidance from HR.
- Remember to focus on the facts without personalizing the situation or succumbing to emotion.

Possible ways in which Rose could realistically react to criticism of her work for the first time:

- Anger
- Frustration
- Disbelief
- Annoyance
- Hostility
- Resentment

Jake would NOT be better off leaving matters as they are because

- Everyone needs feedback, including poor performers.
- Poor performers cannot change if they do not know what aspects of their work are unacceptable.
- Jake's ultimate goal is to help Rose perform to her maximum capacity. This can only be accomplished if she is aware of how her manager currently views her work.

A COMMON MISPERCEPTION ABOUT PERFORMANCE APPRAISALS

Performance appraisals have traditionally been presented to employees as a means to an end, the "end" being a raise. While performance programs can be used as vehicles to support increases, an increasing number of HR specialists strongly recommend separating the timing of appraisals from when salary reviews are conducted. This will preclude an employee who knows there is a direct correlation between his or her rating and the amount of money he or she will receive from tuning out and not listening to the specific observations of their appraiser. Separating the two events minimizes the likelihood that the person being evaluated will be busy calculating how much each rating translates into.

Let's read about a partial performance appraisal meeting between Richard, a first line supervisor in a moving and storage facility, and his manager, Marissa:

Richard is due for his annual performance and salary review. Since he was asked to do a self-evaluation, he knows the four categories for each competency against which he will be measured: exceptional, above expectations, meets expectations, needs improvement. He knows his job fairly well, and thinks he deserves an overall rating of the second highest-level. Marissa has had to speak with him a few times about losing his temper and he has misplaced a few orders, but for the most part he does a good job and he has never been late for work. He hopes his manager agrees with his rating because he has had his eye on a new boat and could really use the extra money.

He enters Marissa's office at the exact scheduled time and takes a seat. Marissa smiles and observes, "I could set my watch by you; you're that punctual." (*What Richard hears: "Great, this is definitely starting off in the right direction. I can just see that new boat now."*)

Marissa begins his review: "Richard, on the whole, I'm extremely pleased with your work over the past year." (*What Richard hears: "This is really good; she's heading for an overall "exceeds expectations" rating for sure."*) "However, as you know, you've had a few problems controlling your temper." (*What Richard hears: "Uh oh, this is bad . . . maybe I'm not getting as much of a raise I was hoping for."*) "In addition, as you know, we've had some customer complaints because you've misplaced a number of orders." (*What Richard hears: "A number of orders? There were a few, but I didn't think it was that big a deal. Maybe I'm not getting that new boat after all."*) Marissa continues: "On the other hand, your employees seem to respect you, except for the ones with whom you've lost your temper, that is; and I can always count on you to be here." (*What Richard hears: "That was a mixed bag; I wish she'd just cut to the chase and tell me how much money I'm getting!"*)

As you can see, Richard is not focused on Marissa's assessment of his performance; to him everything she says translates into how much of a raise he will receive. Richard is preventing Marissa from achieving the overall objective of a performance appraisal: the maximum utilization of every employee's skills, knowledge, and interests. His unwillingness to absorb Marissa's observations of his work to date means that he is unlikely to allow for a discussion about performance expectations, goals, and measurement criteria.

If the prospect of money is removed from this scenario, Richard will be far more likely to be able to focus on Marissa's evaluation of his work to date. Then, together, they can focus on developmental opportunities by examining Richard's strengths and areas requiring improvement. Hence, the recommendation of many HR practitioners: do not discuss salary increases during performance appraisals; ideally, separate the two events by approximately two or three months.

Despite this recommendation, many organizations continue to link appraisals with raises. The reason is simple: it is easier to address performance and salary at the same time than it is to separate them. Employers need to choose between degree of effectiveness and ease.

BENEFITS AND USES OF PERFORMANCE APPRAISALS

Earlier, you read that the most effective performance appraisal programs are those that are viewed as beneficial to employees, appraisers, and the entire organization. Let's explore this more fully while examining benefits and uses of appraisals for these three groups. (See Exhibit 1–2.)

Think About It...

Is there an efficient way to balance the timing of conducting performance appraisals with recommending salary increases that is satisfactory to both employers and employees?

_____ yes _____ no. Explain your answer.

_____

_____

_____

Benefits and Uses for Employees

There are four key ways in which employees can benefit from and use performance appraisals that have nothing to do with money.

1. *Employees receive a clearer understanding of what they are expected to do.* During the performance review process, employees can expect their appraisers to reiterate job expectations, clarify areas of responsibility, and identify any ways in which the scope of the job may have changed. This refresher ensures that both the manager and the employee view the job in the same context.

   For example, for the position of an assistant director of human resources, the appraiser might make the following introductory remarks: "Your primary duties entail recruiting, interviewing, and screening applicants for nonexempt level positions, assisting department heads with hiring decisions, and performing reference checks on potential employees. In addition, over the past several months you've been asked to assist the EEO officer with advising managers on matters of equal employment opportunity and affirmative action as they pertain to the interviewing and hiring process. Is this consistent with your understanding of your primary areas of responsibility?"

   The employee may respond by saying, "Yes, except for the last part. I didn't realize I was going to take on EEO as one of my regular duties; I thought that was just temporary while the EEO representative was out on leave. I don't really think I have enough training to do this on a regular basis." The employee's last statement serves as an excellent segue into the next appraisal benefit for employees.

2. *Employees learn how well they are meeting expectations and the need for training and development.* Once both parties agree on the employer's primary expectations and the employee's areas of responsibility, they can move on to addressing how well the employee has been performing since the time of his or her last review. In the previous example, the appraiser might say, "Overall, you're doing an outstanding job with your recruiting and interviewing tasks. In addition, the department heads have nothing but praise for your selection recommendations. With regard to the

xhibit 1–2

Benefits and Uses of Performance Appraisals

For Employees

- Clear understanding of employer expectations
- How well they are meeting expectations and need for training
- Openly express opinions and concerns
- Pursuit of future goals

For Managers

- Productive utilization of staff
- Isolation of unusual performance
- Enhancement of employer-employee relations
- Clarified areas of responsibility

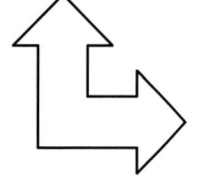
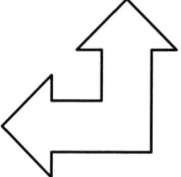
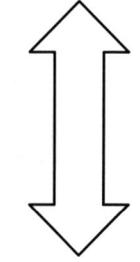

Benefits and Uses of Performance Appraisals

For the Organization

- Consistency
- Communicating strategic vision
- Human resources development and long-term planning
- Equitable salary administration programs
- Future training and development needs
- Employee/job mismatches

EEO tasks, I didn't realize you were under the impression it was temporary: the person who was doing that job isn't coming back. Is this something you see yourself doing on a regular basis?" The employee might then expand upon what she said earlier: "I enjoy the work, but I need a better handle on what I'm doing."

At this point, it would be appropriate for the appraiser and the employee to explore training opportunities together.

3. *Employees are able to openly express opinions and concerns.* Hopefully, employees feel comfortable enough with their managers to consistently express their views. The formal appraisal process, however, affords an atmosphere whereby employees should be encouraged to truly open up and voice their opinions and concerns about anything work-related.

In the previous scenario, the assistant to the director of human resources might comment, "I have to say I feel a little taken advantage of. Obviously you knew the EEO representative wasn't coming back, but you didn't tell me." The appraiser should resist taking this statement personally and engage in a meaningful two-way dialogue with the employee; that way it can lead to the next employee benefit.

4. *Employees can pursue the achievement of future goals.* Employees can benefit greatly from the appraisal process when they are given the opportunity to express their aspirations and pursue growth opportunities. Managers should encourage employees to discuss future goals, even if they are unrelated to their current job. Together, they should map out steps that will ultimately result in the achievement of these goals. These steps may include taking outside courses, shadowing another employee, or working on additional assignments. Setting up dates to discuss progress

---

? **Think About It...**

If your organization has a formal appraisal program do employees . . .

1. Receive a clear understanding of what they are expected to do? _____ yes _____ no

2. Learn how well they are meeting expectations and the need for training and development? _____ yes _____ no

3. Openly express opinions and concerns? _____ yes _____ no

4. Pursue the achievement of future goals? _____ yes _____ no

If your organization does not have a formal appraisal program, or if you answered "no" to any of the previous questions, how do employees . . .

1. Receive a clearer understanding of what they are expected to do?

_____

2. Learn how well they are meeting expectations and the need for training and development?

_____

3. Express opinions and concerns?

_____

4. Pursue the achievement of future goals?

_____

---

toward accomplishing these goals will encourage the employee to be more productive.

Benefits and Uses for Managers

There are four key ways in which managers can benefit from and use performance appraisal programs.

1. *Managers will be able to utilize their staff more productively.* Performance appraisals compel managers to become more aware of each employee's strengths and areas requiring improvement. As a result, they can more effectively determine the best utilization of each person's skills, knowledge, and interests. In turn, this will contribute to a more efficient and productive workflow in the department.

2. *Managers can isolate unusual performance.* Outstanding performers require additional incentives and more challenging assignments to remain on the job. In contrast, poor performers need more guidance and direction, as well as being prevented from interfering with or disrupting the work of others. Performance appraisals help managers identify outstanding and poorly performing employees, as well as isolate specific areas requiring attention. When employees are properly directed, managers are able to focus on developing their own career goals.

3. *Managers can enhance their employer-employee relations as well as focus on honing their managerial abilities.* When conducting performance appraisals, managers need to ask themselves what role their attitude and behavior plays in a particular employee's work performance. For example, if an employee is performing poorly, the appraising manager needs to ask: Was I available for questions? Did I make clear my expectations? Did he or she understand the work assignment? Did I provide realistic deadlines? Was I clear in explaining available resources? Honest answers to questions like these can result in revised approaches to interacting with staff, thereby improving overall employer-employee relations.

4. *Managers can clarify areas of responsibility and work distribution.* Imagine this scenario: you are a manager in your department, with three employees reporting to you. Each employee shares the same title and was hired to perform the same essential functions of their job. From the outset, it

Think About It...

What happens in your organization when one employee's output surpasses that of a colleague who is hired to perform the same tasks?

_____

_____

_____

becomes apparent that Employee A is more inclined to take on extra assignments and stay late as needed. It is not that Employees B and C are unwilling to do their share: they just do not mind if Employee A "steps up to the plate" and takes over. Soon, Employee A, eager to please you and anxious to earn a promotion, is doing more than his share; Employees B and C are fine with this and do less and less work.

The performance appraisal process can help you address this inequity. You may determine that Employee A's title and scope of responsibilities need to change, with an accompanying increase in pay. Or you may decide that Employees B and C need to be held more accountable with Employee A stepping back somewhat. Formally evaluating their respective performance levels will help you determine the best course of action.

Benefits and Uses for the Organization

One of the greatest performance appraisal benefits to an organization has to do with the issue of consistency. Consider, for example, that discrimination complaints often allege that employees with similar performance levels were granted disparate rewards or subjected to different forms of discipline. An effective appraisal system increases the potential for consistency by ensuring that all similarly classified employees are evaluated based on the same criteria. When performance appraisal programs help ensure consistency, some charges of discrimination can be averted.

Organizations also can benefit from and use performance appraisals in communicating their strategic vision with employees. As stated earlier, employee goals should to be as closely aligned as possible with those of the organization. When properly executed, an appraisal system can become a powerful tool for ensuring that employees understand and act on the organization's short- and long-term strategic goals.

Additional benefits and uses of performance appraisals to the organization include:

- Gleaning valuable information for human resources development and long-term planning
- Furnishing data to help establish equitable salary administration programs
- Identifying future training and development needs
- Identifying employees who may have been "mismatched" with their jobs

ELEMENTS OF AN EFFECTIVE PERFORMANCE APPRAISAL SYSTEM

A performance appraisal system should be developed fairly, applied consistently, and evaluated objectively. For this to occur, organizations should make sure that their program meets seven key criteria. These criteria are:

1. *Job related.* A performance program should be founded on criteria that are directly related to the primary duties and responsibilities of a particular job. The criteria should be specific, observable, and measurable. The nature and responsibility level of each position should determine the amount of weight assigned to each factor measured.

2. *Reliable and valid.* To be reliable, a performance appraisal system should yield consistent data regardless of who does the appraising or when it is done. For the system to be valid, there must be a direct correlation between the factors being measured and the critical elements of a particular job. Elements critical to one job may not be relevant at all in another job.

3. *Standardized.* An appraisal program should be standardized in its design and consistent in its administration. All managers and HR practitioners using the system should be given written guidelines and training in its implementation. Organizations should develop effective techniques for monitoring the degree of consistency in implementation.

4. *Practical and workable.* To be effective, a performance appraisal system should be practical, workable, and viewed by all concerned as a helpful tool. It should not be so complex or time-consuming to administer that managers view it as a burden. This can easily occur when forms are very lengthy to complete, multiple approval steps are required, or the system requires a forced distribution of results.

5. *Acceptable to senior management, managers, HR practitioners, and employees.* A performance program should be deemed acceptable by the appraisers and the appraised. Ideally, everyone concerned should have some role in developing the system; many organizations involve employees in the development of criteria for measuring their own performance.

6. *Managerial style should be conducive to employee growth.* In order to create the right climate for a successful performance appraisal system, managers must be encouraging and supportive of their employees' efforts. In addition, they should display confidence in their employees' ability to progress. Managers should ask themselves three key questions about how their style relates to performance management: (1) Do I know how my employees view me? (2) Do I have sufficient confidence in my own skills to encourage the growth and development of others? (3) Do I show interest in my employees and exhibit encouragement for greater accomplishment? If these three questions could be answered affirmatively, the managerial style is considered conducive to employee growth.

7. *Employees should be receptive to suggestions for improving performance.* There is a strong correlation between the overall manager-employee relationship and an employee's receptiveness during the performance appraisal meeting. If this relationship is poor, the employee is not likely to be receptive to even the most well-intentioned suggestions for performance improvement.

? Think About It...

Consider the performance appraisal system in either your current or a past organization. On a scale of 1 to 5, with 1 being the lowest rating and 5 being the highest, how would you rate each of the seven criteria necessary for an effective performance appraisal system?

Job related	1	2	3	4	5
Reliable and valid	1	2	3	4	5
Standardized	1	2	3	4	5
Practical and workable	1	2	3	4	5
Acceptable to everyone	1	2	3	4	5
Managerial style conducive to employee growth	1	2	3	4	5
Employees receptive to suggestions for improvement	1	2	3	4	5

For those criteria that scored lower than 4, what steps could be taken to raise the rating?

_____

_____

_____

RESPECTIVE RESPONSIBILITIES

An effective performance appraisal system requires the cooperation and input of human resources practitioners, managers, and employees. While each has a specific set of responsibilities, every member of HR involved in the process, as well as every manager, is responsible for applying applicable employment laws. Exhibit 1–3 provides a summary of everyone's respective performance appraisal responsibilities.

Human Resources Practitioners

Human resources practitioners are generally responsible for establishing the most appropriate method of evaluating employee performance and for designing the form to be used during the face-to-face meeting. They also typically remind managers when their employees are due for reviews. Once received, HR reviews completed forms, ensuring consistency between comments, ratings, and any recommended action to be taken. If there are any inconsistencies, HR will discuss them with the evaluating manager. In cases where a salary review is tied in with the appraisal, HR is usually responsible for ensuring consistency between the overall evaluations and recommended increases. They will then approve and process the review. HR is also in charge of formally monitoring the performance appraisal system and looking for ways to enhance it.

 **xhibit 1-3**
Respective Performance Appraisal Responsibilities

Human Resources Practitioners

- Applying relevant employment laws
- Establishing the most appropriate method of evaluating employee performance
- Designing performance appraisal forms
- Reminding managers when their employees are due for reviews
- Reviewing completed performance appraisal forms
- Ensuring consistency between comments, ratings, and any recommended action to be taken
- Discussing inconsistencies with the evaluating manager, including those relating to salary recommendations
- Approving and processing the performance appraisal
- Monitoring the performance appraisal system
- Looking for ways to enhance or improve the performance appraisal system

Managers

- Applying relevant employment laws
- Planning and preparing for the performance appraisal meeting, including:

    o Completing the form
    o Preparing the employee for the appraisal meeting

- Recommending a salary increase when raises are tied in with appraisals
- Conducting performance appraisal meetings, emphasizing:

    o The employee's success in meeting agreed-upon goals and objectives since the date of the last review or date of hire
    o Areas requiring improvement
    o How these improvements can be achieved
    o Goals for the upcoming review period
    o Active participation by employees regarding concerns and aspirations

- Providing ongoing coaching
- Providing counseling, as needed

Employees

- Completing a self-evaluation
- Clarifying areas of responsibility
- Asking questions
- Expressing views
- Looking ahead to additional responsibilities and/or job enhancement opportunities

Think About It...

What is the effect on an organization when HR, managers, and employees fail to work together during the performance appraisal process?

_____

_____

What might happen when employees are not asked for their input, via a self-evaluation?

_____

_____

_____

Managers

The planning and preparation stage is an important responsibility of the manager conducting an appraisal. This includes completing the form and preparing the employee for the actual meeting. It may also entail recommending a salary increase. The emphasis during the meeting should be on the employee's success in meeting agreed-upon goals and objectives since the date of the last review or date of hire, areas requiring improvement, how these improvements can be achieved, and goals for the upcoming review period. Appraising managers should also encourage employees to express concerns as well as aspirations. Managers are also responsible for ongoing coaching and counseling, as needed. Coaching may be defined as day-to-day feedback provided by managers; counseling concerns a specific work-related issue. Coaching and counseling will be discussed in depth in Chapter 2.

Employees

Employees are often asked to complete self-evaluations in preparation for the appraisal meeting, filling out the same form as their appraiser. In so doing, they should be prepared to support each rating with specific examples. During the meeting they are responsible for clarifying areas of responsibility, asking questions and expressing views, including those that may differ from their appraisers', and looking ahead to additional responsibilities and/or job enhancement opportunities.

The primary objective of a performance appraisal program is to ensure the maximum utilization of every employee's skills, knowledge, and interests. This results in a more motivated workforce, which, in turn, positively impacts productivity and increases an organization's competitive edge. In addition, employer-employee relations are enhanced, resulting in less strife for managers.

Additional performance appraisal objectives include providing feedback on past performance according to established standards of performance and specific job responsibilities, planning developmental opportunities by identifying employee strengths and areas requiring improvement, and motivating employees to both establish and achieve personal goals that are compatible with organizational goals. Performance objectives can best be accomplished when the organization, its managers, and employees all work together. Lack of clarity and a lack of mutual respect can interfere with the achievement of performance objectives.

Many managers view performance appraisals as a burden, believing they belong in the hands of human resources. This view can be altered if HR helps managers learn to properly complete appraisal forms and conduct appraisal meetings in a maximally effective manner.

Performance appraisals are often viewed as a means to an end, the "end" being a raise. Accordingly, HR specialists strongly recommend separating the timing of appraisals from when salary reviews are conducted.

The most effective performance appraisal programs are those that are considered beneficial to employees, appraisers, and the organization as a whole. Benefits to employees include providing a clearer understanding of what they are expected to do and the opportunity for openly expressing opinions and concerns. Benefits to managers include the ability to utilize their staff more productively and the opportunity for honing their managerial skills. Benefits to the organization include ensuring consistency and communicating company-wide strategic visions.

Performance appraisal systems should be developed fairly, applied consistently, and evaluated objectively. For this to occur, organizations should make sure that their program meets key criteria, including being job related, reliable and valid, standardized, practical and workable, and acceptable to everyone in the organization.

Finally, an effective performance appraisal system requires the cooperation and input of human resources practitioners, managers, and employees. While each has a specific set of responsibilities, every member of HR involved in the process, as well as every manager, is responsible for applying applicable employment laws.

 **Review Questions**

INSTRUCTIONS: Here is the first set of review questions in this self-study course. Answering the questions following each chapter gives you a chance to check your comprehension of concepts as they are presented, reinforces your understanding, and provides you with information that is fundamental to your further study of chapters to come.

As you can see, the answer to each numbered question is printed to the side of the question. Before beginning, conceal the answers in some way, either by folding the page vertically or by placing a sheet of paper over the answers. Then read and answer each question. Compare your answers with those given. For any question you answer incorrectly, make an effort to understand why the answer given is the correct one. You may find it helpful to turn back to the appropriate section of the chapter and review the material about which you were unsure. At any rate, be sure you understand all the review questions before going on to the next chapter.

1. A common misperception about the use of performance appraisals is that they are used primarily as:
    (a) a way for managers to tell employees what they are doing wrong.
    (b) a tool to communicate information about the organization's goals.
    (c) a vehicle to support salary increases.
    (d) an HR instrument designed to support disciplinary action.

    1. (c)

2. To be effective, a performance appraisal system should be practical, workable, and viewed by all as:
    (a) a way to gain a competitive edge.
    (b) a helpful tool.
    (c) the basis for determining salary increases
    (d) a tool to be used in employment lawsuits.

    2. (b)

Do you have questions? Comments? Need clarification?
Call Educational Services at 1-800-225-3215, ext. 600,
or email at ed_svcs@amanet.org.

3. One important area of responsibility for managers during the   3. (b)
performance appraisal process is to:
   (a) establish the most appropriate method of evaluating
       employee performance.
   (b) encourage employees to express concerns as well as
       aspirations.
   (c) conduct a self-evaluation.
   (d) design the form to be used during the face-to-face meeting.

4. The primary objective of a performance appraisal program is to   4. (d)
ensure the maximum utilization of every employee's skills,
knowledge, and:
   (a) contacts.
   (b) ability.
   (c) potential.
   (d) interests.

5. One key way in which employees can benefit from and use   5. (a)
performance appraisals is that they can:
   (a) learn how well they are meeting expectations.
   (b) be groomed for a promotion.
   (c) justify taking more time off from work for good
       performance.
   (d) suggest to managers ways in which the organization can be
       more productive.

2

Coaching and Counseling

focus

Learning Objectives

By the end of this chapter, you should be able to:

- Articulate coaching and counseling objectives and characteristics.
- Distinguish between spontaneous and planned coaching.
- Differentiate between directive and nondirective approaches to counseling.
- Implement managerial coaching and counseling responsibilities with respect to the performance appraisal process.
- Apply effective communication skills when coaching and counseling.
- Measure the effectiveness of communication skills with regard to coaching and counseling.

Felicity was hired as an associate by Twilight Communications, Inc. out of college. She worked hard, and within eighteen months earned a promotion to senior associate; two years later, Felicity was made a manager in charge of eight employees. To make up for her lack of prior managerial experience, she attended workshops and shadowed her predecessor for several weeks, gaining knowledge of key managerial skills such as delegation, decision-making, and time management. With all that she was learning, Felicity was confident that she would succeed in her new role.

Felicity felt everything was going smoothly. She had a keen understanding of the business end of her job and developed what she believed to be a good rapport with her employees. As such, she was surprised to learn during the course of her first managerial performance review that she was perceived as an ineffective coach and counselor. Felicity was taken aback. Coaching struck her as something that belonged on a playing field, and counseling was something social workers and therapists were concerned about. Why or how could she, as a manager, expand her job to encompass being a coach or counselor?

Felicity expressed these thoughts to her supervisor, professing that she did not understand what the terms meant in relation to her job as a manager. He, in turn, responded by assuring her that she was not the first new manager who was stymied upon learning of these additional roles. Together, they agreed to meet the following day, at which time he would explain her coaching and counseling responsibilities. Specifically, he would define and identify each term with regard to their respective objectives and characteristics, provide information concerning different approaches, and offer guidelines for effective coaching and counseling techniques.

"Thanks," murmured Felicity, as she prepared to leave. "One more thing," said her supervisor. "Just as I'm conducting your performance appraisal, you will you be conducting reviews of your employees' performances. Therefore, we'll spend some time tomorrow focusing on the role of coaching and counseling with respect to the performance appraisal process, including the application of some specific communication skills." Felicity turned and asked, "Performance appraisals require coaching and counseling? Have I just been coached and counseled?" Her boss smiled and replied, "Why don't you tell me at the end of tomorrow's meeting?"

Like Felicity, many managers are initially surprised to learn that coaching and counseling are their responsibility. However, once the terms are defined, objectives identified, and characteristics outlined, it becomes clear as to why these two tasks are part of a manager's job.

COACHING

Coaching can be broadly defined as the day-to-day interaction between a manager and his or her employees. The goal of coaching is to regularly offer assistance, support, praise, and constructive criticism. It is most effective when provided on an informal, ongoing basis. Coaching lets employees know what is expected of them and tells them how they are doing. It can help develop needed skills and often heads off potential problems.

Managerial coaching is crucial for making the best use of employees' potential and for keeping them motivated at their jobs. It also contributes to improving the organization's overall productivity. Coaching is as important for top performers as for those employees needing to focus on improving their performance.

Coaching Characteristics

There are ten key coaching characteristics all managers should strive to demonstrate in dealing with their employees:

1. *Approachable.* Whether they need help or want to talk about an idea they have concerning how to proceed with a task, managers need to be viewed as responsive and accessible by their employees; that they can go to their managers at any time for any reason.
2. *Consistent.* To garner and sustain trust and respect from one's employees, managers should strive to conform with and apply organizational policies, procedures, and rules across-the-board.
3. *Dependable.* Nothing shakes an employee's confidence more than feeling uncertain about whether they can count on their manager when needed. Managers who demonstrate that they are reliable are more likely to have maximally effective employer-employee relations.
4. *Discreet.* Managers encounter numerous instances in which they need to show good judgment. This includes knowing when and with whom it is appropriate to share or reveal employee-related information.
5. *Empathetic.* Managers often find themselves in the position of listening to employees' work-related and personal problems. When this happens, they must remain impartial, thereby maintaining an emotional distance so they can best help the employee achieve resolution.
6. *Fair.* Being fair requires managers to be free from self-interest or favoritism. Employees need to believe they will be evaluated or treated the same as anyone else.
7. *Honest.* Managers should try to be straightforward and forthright without being harsh or disrespectful. This is best accomplished by adhering to the facts in all matters calling for both praise and criticism.
8. *Informative.* The most effective managers are those who resist telling employees how to do their jobs; rather, they provide information or resources that will enable employees to solve problems on their own.
9. *Knowledgeable.* "Smart" managers are those who are as clear about what they do not know as they are about what they do know. Smarter still are those who view themselves as lifelong learners.
10. *Respectful.* Savvy managers understand that they cannot demand respect from their employees if they do not offer it. This includes having regard for employees' views, approaches to tasks, requests, and needs.

Spontaneous Coaching

There are two different types of managerial coaching. The first type is spontaneous coaching and requires managers to be attentive and attuned to each employee's individual work habits, routines, and current assignments. Stopping by a worker's desk to say, "Nice job on that monthly report; the summary you wrote clearly explained the sea of numbers preceding it!" is an example of positive spontaneous coaching. Note that the first part of this comment lacks reference to anything specific; left to stand on its own, the generic statement, "nice job on that monthly report" could be perceived as

✎ Exercise: Managerial Coaching Characteristics

Step 1:

Identify each of the following managerial coaching characteristics in terms of how frequently you exhibit them with your employees:

	Always	*Frequently*	*Sometimes*	*Rarely*	*Never*

I am approachable
I am consistent
I am dependable
I am discreet
I am empathetic
I am fair
I am honest
I am informative
I am knowledgeable
I am respectful

Step 2:

Did you indicate that you demonstrate any of the traits "sometimes," "rarely," or "never"? _____ yes _____ no. If so, select one and think about why you do not demonstrate that characteristic "always," or "frequently."

_____

_____

Step 3:

Think about a specific situation in which you were required to demonstrate managerial coaching characteristics. Briefly summarize the incident:

_____

_____

Identify those traits you feel you displayed:

_____ Approachable	_____ Empathetic	_____ Knowledgeable
_____ Consistent	_____ Fair	_____ Respectful
_____ Dependable	_____ Honest	
_____ Discreet	_____ Informative	

Regardless of how effective you believe you were, determine what you might have done to improve that level of effectiveness.

_____

_____

_____

hollow and insincere. Adding details to the observation, however, sends both a clear and sincere message to the employee: that is, the manager read the report and specifically noted the positive impact of the summary.

This example of spontaneous coaching takes less than ten seconds to accomplish; yet in that brief period of time it serves to validate the employee's work and leaves a lasting impression of interest on the part of the manager. If done publicly in front of the employee's coworkers, so much the better. If the manager really wants to drive home the impact of the moment, he or she could follow up with a note or e-mail to human resources for the employee's file. In addition, the manager should note it down in his or her own file for reference when it comes time for the employee's review.

Experts agree that managers should coach often and be generous with praise; it does not cost anything and the rewards can be enormous.

Spontaneous coaching is equally effective when the focus is on performance improvement. While many managers find it daunting to provide corrective feedback, it can be helpful to remember that coaching involves an individual's performance—not their personality. The key to success is to share specific observations leading to a discussion of alternative behaviors or approaches, rather than merely pointing out what is wrong.

Suppose a manager in charge of customer service overhears one of her representatives speaking curtly with a customer. While it may be tempting to issue a reprimand for inappropriate conduct, this will likely serve only to make the employee angry and resentful at being "caught." Instead, the manager can view the unfortunate incident as an opportunity to engage in a dialog with the employee about what happened and how the matter might have been handled more effectively. Care must be taken not to lecture or come across as heavy-handed. Consider this exchange between Jocelyn, a customer service manager, and Becky, one of her representatives. Jocelyn has just walked by Becky's desk and hears the end of Becky's side of a telephone conversation with a customer:

Becky: "I don't know what else you want me to say! I'm sorry your order wasn't filled on time, but there's nothing I can do about it. The person you need to speak with is gone for the day; I'll tell him to call you tomorrow. That's the best I can do!"

Jocelyn: "Sounds like you're having a rough time. What was that about?"

Becky: "That woman was so nasty! She started yelling at me and threatening to cancel her account with us because her delivery didn't arrive on time."

Jocelyn: "I heard the last thing you said to her; I'm guessing she's still pretty upset. I know some customers are harder to deal with than others, but here in customer service we always have to try to end on a positive note. Can you think of anything you might have said to her that would have accomplished that goal?"

Becky: "Not really; I don't like being yelled at and told I'm uncooperative."

Jocelyn: "I guess not, but I wonder if she was really mad at you or frustrated over not having her order on time."

Becky: "She doesn't know me, and I didn't do anything to her, so I guess she was just venting."

Jocelyn: "And . . .?"

Becky: "Well, I guess I could have told her I understand how upset she feels and that I'll do all that I can to help."

Jocelyn: "Do you hear how your tone of voice just changed as soon as you acknowledged that she wasn't mad at you, personally? That enabled you to take a step back and assess the situation. I'll bet you've been in her shoes and just wanted to blow off steam."

Becky: "True . . . I never thought of that."

Jocelyn: "Can you think of any way that you can smooth things over with the customer?"

Becky: "I guess I could call her back and say I want to verify the details of a memo I'm sending to the person who'll be calling her tomorrow."

Jocelyn: "I think that's an excellent idea. And if you use the tone of voice you're using with me right now, I'm pretty sure she won't find you uncooperative."

This type of exchange clearly takes more time and effort than the previous example of positive spontaneous coaching. It is worth the effort, however, since employees are likely to come away understanding that their managers are interested in their performance. As a result, negative behavior is often replaced by constructive conduct.

Think About It...

As a manager, how much time do you devote to spontaneous coaching?

_____

_____

Do you consider yourself equally effective at offering spontaneous positive coaching and spontaneous performance-improvement coaching? _____ yes _____ no. Why or why not?

_____

_____

Planned Coaching

Spontaneous coaching is not always feasible or desirable. For instance, if you observe a situation that calls for performance-improvement coaching, but there are other people around, it is best to wait until you can speak privately to the employee. Just as it is considered good practice to praise an employee in public, extending criticism with others present is ill advised. You do not want to wait too long before addressing an issue that requires attention. Here is where planned coaching comes into play.

Planned coaching allows managers to seek out an opportune time to focus on a situation, but it is still informal in terms of the approach. Here is an example:

Ed, a retail manager, observes one of his sales associates, Serena, talking on her cell phone while at the check-out register. He further observes a customer asking Serena a question, whereupon she holds up her index finger and mouths, "Hold on a minute; I'll be right with you." She finishes her personal call and then turns to the customer. Jed notes that the customer does not seem bothered, but he is. Her actions are inappropriate and he needs to talk with Serena about the matter, but not in front of customers.

He waits until Serena leaves the register for a break and then approaches her. "Serena, I need to speak with you in private for a moment," he states. They go into the cafeteria and find a table separate from the three other people in the room. He begins by making it clear that he knows for a fact that Serena was on her cell phone: "Serena, while you were at the cash register, you were also on your cell phone." He continues, "Do you feel you were able to focus fully on your customers while on the phone?" If Serena answers, "No," Jed can concur; if she says, "Yes," Jed can respond by saying, "Even if that's the case, customers may perceive you as being busy and will be less likely to ask questions. Perhaps some will even consider your behavior rude and hesitate to come back." At this point Jed should allow Serena to respond. She may say she had an emergency, or perhaps she did not think there was a problem. Regardless of what she says, Jed needs to listen. Then

Think About It...

How do you think you would react if Jed reprimanded you in front of customers?

_____

_____

Compare this reaction with your likely response to being asked to step aside to speak privately.

_____

_____

_____

he should have her agree that talking on her cell phone while at the register is unacceptable behavior and that she will not do it again.

This exchange should not take more than a few minutes. The discussion is not intended to be a reprimand, and Jed should allow Serena to extend her break time by the amount of time it took to talk with her. The matter is important and calls for immediate attention, but it is not serious.

COUNSELING

When attempts to alter an employee's performance through one or two planned coaching exchanges fail, the manager must shift his or her role to that of counselor.

Counseling Characteristics

Counseling is the structured interaction between managers and their employees, focusing more keenly on particular work-related issues. The process enables employees to examine their behavior, explore alternative ways of performing, and review the possible consequences of each alternative. The primary goal of counseling is to help employees achieve a maximum level of productivity in accordance with specified job duties, policies, and procedures.

To illustrate, let's return to the scenario between Jed and Serena. As you recall, Jed had overheard Serena speaking on her cell phone while helping a customer. He spoke with her briefly, making clear that the behavior she exhibited was unacceptable. Let's assume Serena agreed and committed to not using her cell phone during working hours. Three weeks pass since the initial incident. Late one afternoon, Jed is once again in the store and sees Serena on her cell phone while at the register. Her voice is loud, making it clear that the conversation is of a personal, non-urgent, nature. When Serena sees Jed she quickly hangs up. Jed quietly comments, "Serena, I thought we had an understanding about this." She nods, seemingly in agreement.

Jed returns to the store a few days later, believing that the matter with Serena has been resolved. As he approaches Serena's register, he overhears her again on the cell phone. Her tone is more hushed, but it is obvious she is talking with a friend and making plans for after work. Jed knows the matter now requires formal counseling. He further understands that he has a choice of utilizing one of two approaches: directive or nondirective counseling.

Directive Counseling

With the directive approach, managers identify the problem, tell the employee why it is a problem, and then tell the employee what he or she needs to do to rectify the matter. Managers are also likely to include a time-line and the communication is usually much one-way. Here's an example:

"Serena, I called you in here to discuss your use of a cell phone during working hours. As you recall, I spoke with you about this three weeks ago;

since that time, I've overheard you on your cell phone with customers nearby on two separate occasions. This behavior is in direct violation of store policy and must stop immediately. If you have to make a personal phone call, I expect you to do so during breaks or lunch. You need to comply immediately. If I catch you on the cell phone again I will be forced to write you up."

By utilizing a directive counseling approach, managers are in complete control, steering the method for resolving the employee's problem. Since this technique leaves little room for dispute or confusion, it may initially appear to ensure a positive outcome; unfortunately, it rarely does. In fact, the directive approach often results in damaged employer-employee relations, often reaching a point of non-repair. To make matters worse, the impact of the tainted manager/employee relationship frequently spills over into the workplace, creating disharmony with other workers, and ultimately impacting productivity. This happens because employees often resent being told they have a problem and further resent being told how to solve it.

Nondirective Counseling

The nondirective counseling approach calls for a partnership between a manager and an employee, with each having a specified role. While it is more structured than the directive approach, it is far less rigid in its application. Experts believe that the nondirective approach is more likely to result in positive change because the employee has greater control over his or her behavior. The specific sequence of nondirective counseling steps is as follows (Exhibit 2–1):

Step 1: The manager begins by stating the purpose of the counseling session. For instance, "Serena, I called you in here to discuss your use of a cell phone during working hours." Note that this introductory statement is identical to that used to illustrate the directive approach.

Step 2: The manager then defines and recaps the problem: "As you recall, I spoke with you about this three weeks ago; since that time, I have personally overheard you on your cell phone with customers nearby on three separate occasions." Again, the language is the same as that used in the directive approach example. Similarities between the two approaches are about to change, however.

Think About It...

Think about a time when someone said you were doing something wrong and then proceeded to tell you how to correct your behavior. How did you react?

_____

_____

_____

Exhibit 2–1

Seven Steps of Nondirective Counseling

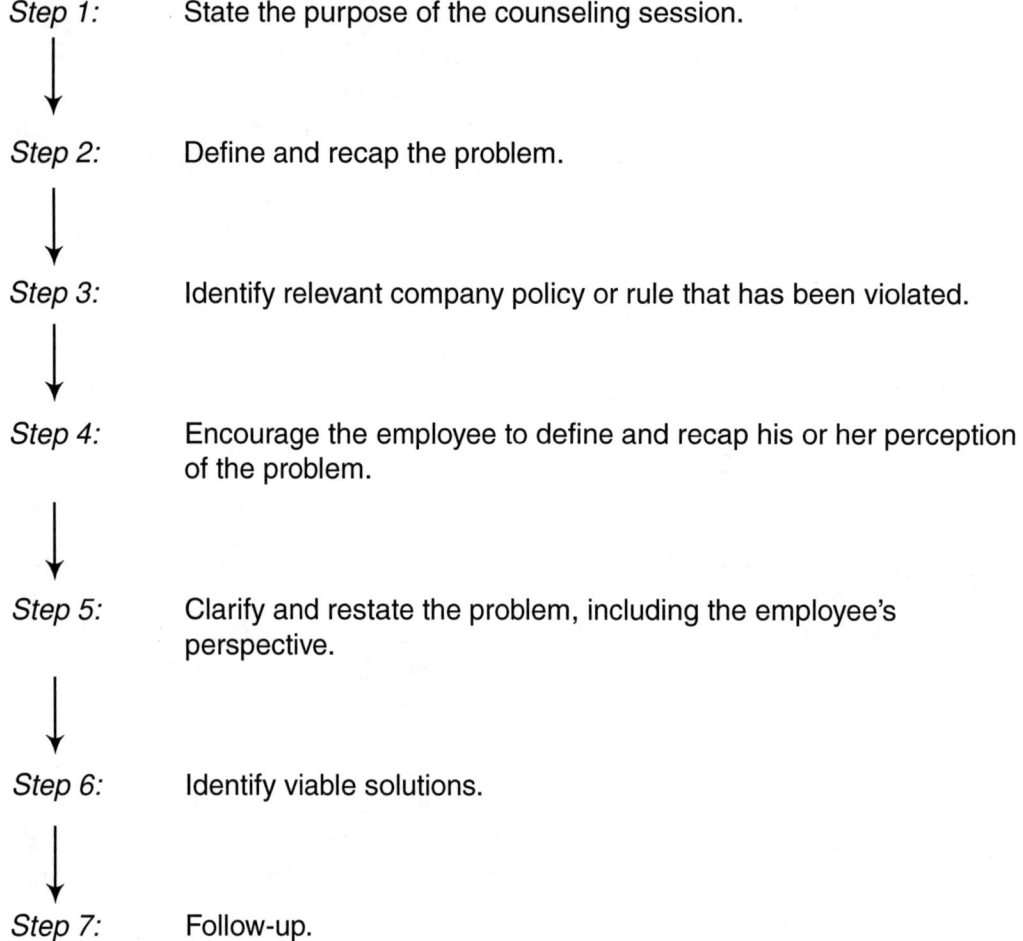

Step 1:   State the purpose of the counseling session.

Step 2:   Define and recap the problem.

Step 3:   Identify relevant company policy or rule that has been violated.

Step 4:   Encourage the employee to define and recap his or her perception of the problem.

Step 5:   Clarify and restate the problem, including the employee's perspective.

Step 6:   Identify viable solutions.

Step 7:   Follow-up.

Step 3: The next step calls for managers to identify any relevant company policy or rule that the employee has violated. With the directive approach, Jed began by saying, "This behavior is in direct violation of store policy and must stop immediately."

Here is where we begin to see a distinction between the two forms of counseling. Using the nondirective approach, Jed would first cite the specific policy Serena has violated: "Serena, on page 27 of your Employee Handbook, it states that employees are not permitted to use the phone to make or receive personal calls during working hours, except in the event of an emergency." He would then continue by adding, "The Phone Use section of your Handbook explains that employees can make personal calls during breaks or on their lunch hour."

By referencing a specific portion of the employee handbook, Jed draws Serena's focus to something tangible and impersonal, making it more difficult for her to become defensive.

Step 4: Now it is the employee's turn to express his or her opinion about the situation. In the scenario between Jed and Serena, Jed could turn to Serena and simply state, "I'd like to hear what you have to say about this." She might respond with, "I really don't see why this is a problem. I'm perfectly capable of talking on the phone while working the register. Have any of the customers complained? Have I made any mistakes? I don't get why this is a big deal."

A dialogue between the manager and the employee should then follow this interaction. The manager should remain objective throughout this exchange, adhering to the facts, the content of the policy violated, and the impact of the violation on the workplace. The employee should be encouraged to express his or her views, as long as the discussion does not escalate into an argument. When it appears that both parties have expressed themselves, it is time for the manager to move on to Step 5.

Step 5: At this point the manager needs to clarify and restate the problem, as well as to credit the employee's perspective. Hence, Jed might say, "Serena, I understand you feel strongly about being able to talk on the cell phone while doing your job without error or complaint. It may very well be that you can; however, the fact remains that the store has a specific policy about using the phone during working hours and everyone needs to adhere to it."

Notice that the manager remains objective and does not reference his personal feelings. The directive counseling approach, on the other hand, had Jed using "I" three times: ". . . *I* expect you to do so during breaks or lunch. You need to comply immediately. If *I* catch you on the cell phone again *I* will be forced to write you up."

Step 6: Now it is time to come up with a viable solution to the problem. The responsibility is that of the employee, although the manager is responsible for eliminating those solutions that are unacceptable. For example, an employee with a chronic punctuality problem may suggest that she be permitted to start work one hour later. If flextime is not offered in your organization then this is not a viable option. Managers are also responsible for ultimately approving the approach selected by the employee. This stage of the nondirective approach to counseling, then, is a joint effort between the employee and the manager.

To illustrate by way of the scenario between Serena and Jed, Serena might say, "I can't say that I agree with the policy about personal phone calls, but I guess I'll just have to comply; I'll try to make my calls during lunch or breaks. But you have to understand—sometimes my mom calls when I'm at the register, and since she's been in and out of the hospital lately I need to make sure she's all right." Jed might reply, "How about this: explain to your mom that you can't talk during working hours, unless it's an urgent situation. That way if she does call, you'll know it's pressing. We can certainly show flexibility in the event of an emergency. Now, what can you do about other incoming phone calls?"

Serena thinks for a moment, then replies: "Well, I guess I can keep my phone on mute and check it every once in awhile to see if my mom or anyone else has called; if it's a friend I can call them back during breaks or lunch. Is that okay?" Jed smiles and says, "Yes, Serena, that sounds like a workable solution. Let's meet again in a week to talk about how it's going."

Step 7: The final stage of nondirective counseling is the follow-up. Depending on the nature of the infraction, managers should arrange to meet with employees in one to two weeks after they have had a chance to implement agreed-upon changes. If needed, they can agree on additional, subsequent checkpoint dates.

✎ Exercise: Nondirective Counseling

Consider this scenario: You work as a manager for a security and alarm company and are in charge of four employees, two of whom work the night shift. One of the two night workers has started showing up late for his shift, forcing the day worker to stay behind until his replacement shows up. Since you work during the day, you do not have firsthand knowledge of this happening, but you learn of it when the day worker complains to you.

When you examine the night shift employee's time cards you are able to confirm that he has, in fact, reported late to work on three occasions during the past week. You stay late the next day and speak with the employee when he arrives, expressing your concern about his punctuality. He assures you that it will not happen again. A week goes by and you check his time cards: he has been late again twice. You decide the matter calls for a nondirective counseling approach.

As the manager in this scenario, identify the steps you will take in addressing this matter. Be specific.

Step 1:

_____

_____

Step 2:

_____

_____

Step 3:

_____

_____

Step 4:

_____

_____

Step 5:

_____

_____

Step 6:

_____

_____

Step 7:

_____

_____

HINTS, SUGGESTIONS, AND SOME ANSWERS

Step 1: Set up a counseling session with the employee and state its purpose: "I called you in to discuss your continued problem with punctuality."

Step 2: Define and recap the problem: "As you recall, I spoke with you about this last week and you assured me that you would not come to work late again. Since then you've been late twice."

Step 3: Identify the company policy or rule that the employee has violated: "Page 21 of your Employee Handbook explains the importance of employees reporting to work on time. This is especially important when your coworker from the day shift is waiting for you to arrive so he or she can leave."

Step 4: "I'd like to hear what you have to say about this." Depending on what the employee says, engage in a dialogue with the employee. Throughout the exchange, ask yourself: Am I remaining objective? Am I adhering to the facts, the content of the policy violated, and the impact of the violation on the workplace? Am I encouraging the employee to express his views?

Step 5: Clarify and restate the problem, as well as crediting the employee's perspective: "I understand you fully intend to arrive at work on time, but that sometimes the bus breaks down; however, the fact remains that the company has a specific policy about punctuality."

Step 6: Help the employee come up with a viable solution by eliminating alternatives that are unacceptable and ultimately approving the approach he selects. For example, the employee may be able to take an alternative mode of transportation to ensure arriving at work on time.

Step 7: Meet with the employee in one or two weeks to determine whether he has resolved his punctuality problem. If necessary, agree on additional checkpoint dates.

Managerial Coaching and Counseling Responsibilites and the Performance Appraisal Process

There is a golden rule when it comes to coaching and counseling: whenever possible, managers should talk with employees at the time an incident occurs, or as shortly thereafter as possible. When it comes to performance appraisals, the rule becomes platinum: nothing said during a performance appraisal session should ever come as a surprise to an employee. These two rules are intrinsically linked: that is, when employees enter their managers' office for the annual performance review, they should have a clear idea as to how they are going to be evaluated. If they have consistently been doing well, they should know this as a result of informal, ongoing praise offered by their manager through the year. If there have been performance-related problems, they will be already be aware of these problems as a result of coaching and more structured counseling sessions.

To illustrate, we will return to the coaching offered by Jocelyn to Becky, a customer service representative, and the counseling provided Serena, a sales associate, by Jed. Several months have passed in each scenario, and it is now time for their respective annual performance appraisals. Let's begin with Jocelyn and Becky:

As you recall, Jocelyn was walking by Becky's desk when she overheard the end of Becky's side of a telephone conversation with a customer. Becky was agitated with what she perceived to be the customer's unreasonable demands, and made clear these feelings to the customer. Jocelyn spoke with her immediately after the incident, and Becky acknowledged that she could have been more tactful in her approach. In addition, she offered to attempt to rectify the matter by following up with the customer the next day.

During the portion of Becky's performance appraisal pertaining to challenging customer service issues, Jocelyn should raise the matter of Becky's handling of that customer, but not as a focal point involving criticism. Jocelyn can refer to it as an example of how she effectively converted negative behavior into a positive outcome. It becomes a recap, as opposed to a new topic. More significantly, it becomes a positive reference, setting the tone for the rest of the review.

The matter concerning Serena is more complicated: what started out as coaching on Jed's part escalated into counseling. Let us assume Jed opted for the nondirective method of counseling. We can also further assume that he last spoke with Serena about her inappropriate use of her cell phone during working hours three months prior to her annual performance appraisal, and that there have been no additional incidences since that time. At some point during Serena's performance appraisal meeting, Jed will raise the matter of her cell phone use, but not to chastise her. He will review what happened, identify the steps she took toward preventing the matter from occurring again, and commend her on successfully resolving the matter.

Now let us assume that at the time of her performance appraisal meeting the matter concerning Serena's inappropriate cell phone use remains unresolved. Jed now needs to take a different approach. He will review the steps taken to date, including all informal and formal discussions, as well as documentation, if any. He will then comment on the impact of Serena's failure to amend her behavior on her overall evaluation. If Jed's company ties increases in with appraisals, he may address how Serena's wrongdoing affects her raise, as well. Most importantly, the focus needs to be on what Serena intends to do to correct matters. In addition, formal disciplinary action may be warranted.

APPLY EFFECTIVE COMMUNICATION SKILLS TO COACHING AND COUNSELING

In order to integrate coaching and counseling with the overall performance appraisal process, managers should strive to hone two important communication skills: verbal and written. In addition, managers need to be aware of body language (their own and that of their employees), and active listening. (These last two aspects of communication will be discussed in Chapter 6 as an integral part of the face-to-face meeting.)

Perhaps the most critical overall concept for managers to keep in mind with regard to these verbal and written communication skills is that there is always a sender and a receiver. The manager is not always the sender: that is, effective verbal or written communication is a two-way process. In addition, the receiver not only "hears" the message, he or she also provides feedback; such feedback confirms understanding and also relays information back to the sender.

Verbal Communication Skills

Here are ten guidelines for applying verbal communication skills as they relate to coaching and counseling in particular, and to the performance appraisal process overall:

- Ask questions instead of making statements whenever possible
- Express ideas concisely
- Organize ideas clearly
- Periodically summarize or paraphrase the employee's understanding of what has been discussed
- Respond in ways that convey interest in what the employee is saying
- Select stories or examples to illustrate a relevant point
- Speak clearly
- Tailor content of speech to the level and experience of your employee
- Use appropriate grammar and choice of words
- Use non-threatening language

Managers are also advised to be specific when it comes to complimenting performance, providing constructive criticism, helping employees set goals, setting measurable timelines, and identifying resources. In addition, they should be flexible when it comes to negotiating alternative approaches to resolving conflicts.

We will apply these verbal communication skills to the performance appraisal meeting between Jed and Serena. As you recall, we considered two possible scenarios about Serena's performance: first, that she had corrected the misuse of her cell phone during working hours and no further action was needed; second, that she was still receiving and making calls while on the job, necessitating additional intervention by Jed. We will presume the second situation prevails. We will further assume that the performance appraisal is underway and that we are now addressing only that portion specifically dealing with Serena's continued violation of the company's phone policy. The applicable verbal communication skill is cited in parenthesis.

Jed: "Serena, we now need to address your continued use of a cell phone to make and receive personal calls while working at the register (speak clearly). Could you please recap your understanding of what we've discussed about this up until now (ask questions instead of making statements)?"

Serena: "Well, you told me it's against policy to use my phone for personal calls while I'm on the floor; that I could do that on my breaks and during lunch. And then I told you that my mom is sick and that sometimes she needs me during the day. So you agreed that I could talk with her if there's an emergency, but otherwise I couldn't talk with anyone. Oh, and also, I said I'd keep my phone on mute."

Jed: "That's how I remember our last discussion. Before we go any further, I hope your mom is feeling better (respond in ways that convey interest in what the employee is saying)."

Serena: "Yes, much better; thanks for asking."

Jed: "I'm glad to hear it; I know how concerned you've been. My dad was ill last year and I understand how difficult it is when you're trying to concentrate on your job and still care for a loved one. My boss sat down with me, just as I sat with you, so we could come up with a viable solution (select stories or examples to illustrate a relevant point). How successful do you feel you've been with implementing the solution you agreed to (ask questions instead of making statements)?"

Serena: "I started out O.K., but then I guess I sort of slipped. I know I said I'd keep my phone on mute, but I started to think about the policy and thought it really didn't make much sense since I wasn't hurting anyone and I was still able to get my work done."

Jed: "Is it safe to say, then, that you remembered our agreement and chose to sidestep it (periodically summarize or paraphrase the employee's understanding of what's been discussed)?"

Serena: "The rule seems too strict."

Jed: "The rule applies to all employees and exists so we can best serve our customers (organize ideas clearly; express ideas concisely). Serena, as we've discussed, your work is otherwise excellent: customers respond positively to you and you get along well with coworkers. With the exception of this matter with the cell phone, you've responded well to past suggestions for improvement, such as in how you deal with questions concerning inventory. The continued misuse of the phone is a problem, however; one that is, unfortunately, going to result in disciplinary action, and impact future job opportunities and salary increases if left unresolved. Let's focus on where we're going with this and try to take care of the matter, once and for all. We need to set an outside date for when this violation ends. Let's consider, also, if there are alternatives or resources we didn't consider during our counseling session (use non-threatening language; tailor content of speech to the level and experience of employee; use appropriate grammar and choice of words)."

In addition to applying the ten guidelines, Jed complimented Serena's performance, provided constructive criticism, and was prepared to help her set a goal with a measurable timeline as well as identifying resources. He remains flexible with regard to whatever corrective approach Serena opts for, but is fixed in maintaining that she must comply with the company's policy.

Written Communication Skills

The written performance appraisal will receive in-depth consideration in Chapter 5. We do need to mention other forms of written communication and their overall impact on the performance appraisal process. In particular, managers should avoid excessive reliance on electronic communication as a substitute for verbal interaction with their employees. While undeniably convenient and efficient, e-mails and instant messages are not acceptable replacements for face-to-face contact. These channels do not allow for important qualities, such as voice inflection and tone, which more fully communicate to an employee the intent of your message. Indeed, over-reliance on electronic communication can result in misunderstandings and otherwise impair employer-employee relations.

 **Think About It...**

Given Jed's approach, how do you think Serena is likely to respond?

Is there anything additional Jed might have conveyed verbally that might ensure cooperation on Serena's part? Please explain.

It is unrealistic to suggest that managers refrain altogether from communicating electronically with their employees during the performance appraisal process. The key to success lies in adhering to these guidelines:

- *Exercise care when copying others.* E-mail makes it easy to forward copies to everyone you know; before copying others, however, stop and ask yourself who would benefit from receiving your message to an employee. In addition, consider the possible impact on the employee of your e-mail being read by others.
- *Follow-up whatever you write with face-to-face contact.* If you send an employee an e-mail advising them that they are late with a report, stop by their office to discuss the matter. This action makes the communication two-way, thereby affording the employee an opportunity to explain and/or ask questions.
- *Send your e-mail only after carefully thinking through how your written words are likely to be interpreted.* Write your message and then read it from the perspective of the employee. Be certain there is no room for misinterpretation.
- *Treat the subject with the importance it deserves.* Matters concerning performance appraisals are inherently important. Accordingly, offhand remarks and attempts at humor should be avoided.
- *Use an appropriate business writing style.* Many people think that communicating via e-mail means all writing rules fall by the wayside. Whether you follow this practice in your casual correspondence is up to you, but e-mails concerning performance appraisals call for appropriate business writing style. This includes using correct spelling, grammar, and punctuation; expressing ideas clearly and concisely; and applying concrete, specific language.
- *Use regular font.* Bold print, italics, all capital letters, drop caps, borders, shading, symbols, captions, pictures, excessive sized print, or special effects, such as strikethrough, outline or shadows, are inappropriate when it comes to performance-related e-mails.

Here are two examples of written e-mail communications:

Example #1: hey john, this is your somewhat annoyed boss, artie! Where's the pana corp report that was due friday????????????? what happened, too much partying over the weekend? (HAHA) come on buddy, this is the second time you've been late with your work in the last three weeks. I DON'T WANT TO HAVE TO WRITE YOU UP! plus your performance appraisal is around the corner – you want a raise, don't you? listen – you're gonna want my job one day so work with me here! i need that report by 5:00 – no excuses. i'm sending a copy of this to jack so he knows the report is on its way. don't make a liar out of me!

Example #2: John, I still haven't received the Pana Corp. report that was due on Friday. If you recall, we spoke about the importance of meeting deadlines when we met a few weeks ago, and you assured me that you would work on your time management. Let's meet later this afternoon; I'm interested in hearing what steps you plan on taking to ensure the timely delivery of future work. I'll come by your office at 3:30 so we can talk. Meanwhile, if you need anything to expedite the delivery of the Pana Corp. report, let me know. See you later.

✎ Exercise: Written Communication

Rate the effectiveness of the two e-mails by assigning a number from 1–5, with 1 being the most effective and 5 being the least effective, according to these criteria:

	Ex. #1	Ex. #2
Copying others	_____	_____
Follow-up with face-to-face contact	_____	_____
Think about how written words are likely to be interpreted	_____	_____
Treat the subject with the importance it deserves	_____	_____
Use an appropriate business writing style	_____	_____
Use regular font	_____	_____

Based on your ratings, how would you assess the overall effectiveness of

Example #1? _____

Example #2? _____

HINTS, SUGGESTIONS, AND SOME ANSWERS

	Ex. #1	Ex. #2
Copying others	5	1
Follow-up with face-to-face contact	5	1
Think about how written words are likely to be interpreted	5	1
Treat the subject with the importance it deserves	5	1
Use an appropriate business writing style	5	1
Use regular font	5	1

Based on your ratings, how would you assess the overall effectiveness of Example #1?

Example #1 is completely ineffective. Artie inappropriately sends a copy of the e-mail to someone else and fails to suggest a face-to-face follow-up. The tone of the e-mail reads like a veiled threat, the attempt at humor is inappropriate, as is the periodic use of all capital letters.

Example #2 is a well-written e-mail. There is no mention of sending a copy to anyone else, a face-to-face meeting is referenced, the subject matter is treated as important, the writing is professional and to the point, and there are no distracting fonts, characters, or text effects.

MEASURE THE EFFECTIVENESS OF COMMUNICATION SKILLS

Knowing that you are applying effective verbal and written communication skills is critical; however, you also need to know that whatever you are communicating is having the desired impact.

Measuring the effectiveness of communication skills begins with having a clear understanding of what you want to achieve followed by conveying this objective to the employee. In instances resulting in coaching or counseling, managers want their employees to improve performance. But that is not specific enough: Jocelyn wants Becky to be more courteous in dealing with irate customers, Jed wants Serena to stop using her cell phone during work, and Artie wants John to turn in his work on time. These are specific, straightforward, measurable objectives that can be clearly and concisely communicated to employees.

Working together with their employees, managers should set a timeline for accomplishing a given goal. Begin by identifying where you are now; then establish points along the way for progress reports. For instance, Becky could supply Jocelyn with feedback from a customer who was pleased with how she handled her complaint and Artie could complement John for turning in his next report two days early. These are both measurable results.

Finally, measurable results are more likely to continue when managers provide ongoing feedback and encouragement. In this regard, it helps to have a communication plan whereby you map out a timeline for providing praise and constructive criticism. Remember, praising an employee in front of his or her colleagues can be especially effective.

Over a period of time, you will be able to do a follow-up measurement and determine if more work needs to be done. Is Becky consistently patient with irate customers? Has Serena stopped making and receiving personal calls during working hours? Is John better able to meet deadlines?

✎ Exercise: Measuring the Effectiveness of Communication Skills

Think about a specific coaching or counseling situation in which you wanted an employee to improve his or her performance; respond to the following questions:

Did you have a clear understanding of what you wanted to achieve? _____ yes _____ no. Were your objectives measurable? _____ yes _____ no

Did you convey this objective to the employee involved? _____ yes _____ no. Were you specific, straightforward, and concise? _____ yes _____ no

Did you work together with the employee to set a timeline for accomplishing the goal? _____ yes _____ no

Did you establish points along the way for progress reports reflecting measurable results? _____ yes _____ no

Did you provide ongoing feedback and encouragement? _____ yes _____ no

Did you have a communication plan mapping out a timeline for providing praise? _____ yes _____ no

Did you take advantage of opportunities to praise the employee in front of his or her coworkers? _____ yes _____ no

Did you do a follow-up measurement and determine if more work needs to be done? _____ yes _____ no

If you answered "no" to any of these questions, consider what you might have done differently to ensure more productive results.

_____

_____

_____

Coaching is the day-to-day interaction between managers and employees. The goal of coaching is to regularly provide assistance, support, praise, and constructive criticism. Managerial coaching is crucial for making the best use of employees' potential and for keeping them motivated at their jobs. There are two different forms of managerial coaching: spontaneous and planned. Spontaneous coaching requires managers to be attentive and attuned to each employee's individual work habits, routines, and current assignments. It can involve praise or corrective feedback. Planned coaching allows managers to seek out a specific time to focus on a matter requiring correction.

When attempts to alter an employee's performance through one or two planned coaching exchanges fail, managers must shift their role to that of counselor. Counseling is the structured interaction between managers and their employees, focusing more keenly on particular work-related issues. Directive counseling requires managers to identify the problem, tell the employee why it is a problem, and then inform the employee as to what he or she needs to do to rectify the matter. Nondirective counseling calls for a partnership between a manager and an employee. It is more structured than the directive approach, but less rigid in application.

There are two important rules when it comes to coaching and counseling with regard to performance appraisals: first, coaching and counseling should, as much as possible, take place at the time an incident occurs; and second, nothing said during a performance appraisal session should ever come as a surprise to an employee.

In order to effectively apply coaching and counseling to the overall performance appraisal process, managers should strive to hone their verbal and written communication skills. To be meaningful, communication should be two-way.

To measure the effectiveness of communication skills managers are advised to have a clear understanding of what they want to achieve, convey this objective to the employee, work together to establish a timeline for accomplishing a given goal, and provide ongoing feedback and encouragement.

Review Questions

1. The nondirective counseling approach calls for a partnership between a manager and an employee, with each having a specified role. Experts believe the nondirective approach is more likely to result in positive change because:
   (a) the manager has greater control over the employee's behavior.
   (b) the manager steers the method for resolving the employee's problem.
   (c) the technique leaves little room for dispute or confusion.
   (d) the employee has greater control over his or her behavior.

2. Planned coaching allows managers to seek out an opportune time to focus on a situation, but is still:
   (a) informal.
   (b) direct.
   (c) nondirect.
   (d) spontaneous.

3. The platinum rule of coaching and counseling is that nothing said during a performance appraisal session should:
   (a) be revealed in advance.
   (b) be shared with anyone else.
   (c) have anything to do with a raise.
   (d) ever come as a surprise to the employee.

4. Measuring the effectiveness of communication skills begins with having a clear understanding of what you want to achieve, followed by:
   (a) offering feedback and encouragement.
   (b) conveying this objective to the employee.
   (c) a written report.
   (d) setting a timeline for accomplishing a given goal.

5. When it comes to complementing performance, providing constructive criticism, and helping employees establish goals and set measurable timelines, managers need to be:
   (a) spontaneous.
   (b) direct.
   (c) specific.
   (d) creative.

1. (d)

2. (a)

3. (d)

4. (b)

5. (c)

Do you have questions? Comments? Need clarification?
Call Educational Services at 1-800-225-3215, ext. 600,
or email at ed_svcs@amanet.org.

Establishing Standards of Performance

focus

Learning Objectives

By the end of this chapter, you should be able to:

* Describe the legal parameters of measuring performance.
* Explain the critical factors inherent in all appraisal methods and choose the one most suitable for your organization.
* Use position descriptions effectively when setting standards of performance.
* Recognize the impact of disciplinary action and documentation on performance standards.
* Assess the effectiveness of forms as an instrument in the appraisal process.

I recently received an e-mail from a former student who now works in the human resources department of a computer services company. She said that one of her responsibilities was to help evaluate the effectiveness of their current performance appraisal program, including a review of how to best establish standards of performance. She had remembered how I had said that appraisals are deemed purposeful only when they reflect certain factors; unfortunately, she could not remember what several of those factors were. Here is my response to her:

"Hi, Melanie—It was good to hear from you. You're correct in recalling that there are some key factors that an organization should consider when establishing performance standards. Actually, there are five critical elements: (1) knowing and working within relevant legal parameters, (2)

49

Think About It...

Concerning your organization's approach to establishing standards of performance . . .

Does your organization factor in legal considerations? _____ yes _____ no

How long has your organization been using its current appraisal method?

_____

Has the effectiveness of your appraisal method ever been challenged? _____ yes _____ no

How often are your position descriptions reviewed for accuracy?

_____

Does your organization have a progressive disciplinary process with specific identified steps? _____ yes _____ no

Are managers advised about how to document performance? _____ yes _____ no

On a scale of 1 to 10, with 1 being most effective and 10 being least effective, how useful are your company's appraisal forms?

1   2   3   4   5   6   7   8   9   10

Support your selection.

_____

_____

selecting an appraisal method that reflects the culture of a particular work environment, (3) utilizing position descriptions that accurately reflect a job's requirements and responsibilities, (4) considering the role of a company's disciplinary process and accompanying documentation, and (5) effectively using performance appraisal forms. By establishing these five factors as the foundation for evaluating actual employee performance, any organization—regardless of size, composition, or product—will be better able to gauge individual strengths and areas requiring improvement. In addition, employees can better establish work-related goals that mesh with those of their organization.

I hope this information proves to be helpful; keep me posted."

After I sent my reply and thought about what I had written, it occurred to me that many organizations complain about employee performance and look for a "cure" through training. Training is often called for, but it should never be viewed as a substitute for an ineffective appraisal process. Consider this: If standards of performance are incorrectly and/or incompletely identified, how can an employee's work be accurately evaluated?

LEGAL PARAMETERS OF MEASURING PERFORMANCE

Managers often tune out at the mention of the word "legal," believing that it does not fall within the scope of their responsibilities. While no one expects managers to be legal experts, organizations have increasingly come to rely on them to be familiar with and implement relevant legislation regarding employer-employee relations. Such is the case when it comes to performance appraisals. Managers should be able to identify and apply those laws that relate to standards of performance, turning to their human resources and legal departments for assistance, as needed.

Key Legislation

Familiarity with legal parameters that relate performance appraisals begins with an overview of relevant fair employment laws. While these laws encompass many facets of employer-employee relations, they are often solely associated with employment and overlooked when it comes to performance appraisals. As such, managers are often unaware of the role of legislation in the evaluation process. Simply stated, what is illegal during the hiring stage is still illegal when it comes to the evaluation process. Let's look at some of these laws more closely, as well as their possible impact on the workplace. Note that the information contained in this chapter is not intended to represent legal advice and is current as of this writing.

Federal Legislation

The following are highlights of major federal fair employment laws. Employers are urged to obtain a copy of each of these and other laws relevant to their places of business. Unless otherwise noted, copies of the laws may be obtained from:

> Equal Employment Opportunity Commission (EEOC)
> Department of Labor
> 1801 L Street NW
> Washington, D.C. 20507
> Phone: 202-663-4900
> http://www.eeoc.gov/

Civil Rights Act of 1964. This is probably the best-known piece of civil rights legislation and the most widely used, in that it protects several classes of people and pertains to many employment situations, including performance appraisals. Title VII of this Act prohibits discrimination on the basis of race, color, religion, sex, or national origin in all matters of employment. Criteria for coverage under Title VII include any company doing business in the United States with fifteen or more employees. Title VII does not regulate the employment practices of U.S. companies employing American citizens outside of the United States. Violations are monitored by the EEOC.

Plaintiffs in Title VII suits generally need not prove intent; rather, they may challenge apparently neutral policies having a discriminatory effect.

Equal Pay Act of 1963. This act requires equal pay for men and women performing substantially equal work. The work must be of comparable skill, effort, and responsibility, performed under similar working conditions. Coverage applies to all aspects of the employment process including increases connected with performance appraisals. This law protects women only; men who feel they are being discriminated against in matters of pay may claim violation of Title VII. Criteria for coverage are at least two employees.

Age Discrimination in Employment Act of 1967 (ADEA). As originally written, ADEA protected individuals from ages 40 to 70. Now, most private sector and federal, state, and local government employees cannot be discriminated against regardless of how old they may be. ADEA also pertains to employees of employment agencies and labor organizations, as well as to U.S. citizens working outside the United States. ADEA contains an exemption for bona fide executives or high-level policy makers who may be retired as early as age 65, if they have been employed at that level for the preceding two years and meet certain criteria, including: exercising discretionary powers on a regular basis; the authority to hire, promote, and terminate employees; a primary duty to manage an entire organization, department, or subdivision. The general criterion for coverage under ADEA is employment of at least twenty employees.

Americans with Disabilities Act of 1990 (ADA). The ADA prohibits all employers, including privately owned businesses and local governments, from discriminating against individuals with disabilities. Exempt are the federal government, government-owned corporations, Native American tribes, and bona fide tax-exempt private membership clubs. Religious organizations are permitted to give preference to the employment of their own members. In addition, the law requires every kind of establishment to be accessible to and usable by persons with disabilities. This legislation pertains to employers with fifteen or more employees and is monitored by the EEOC.

Under the ADA, the term *disability* is defined as a physical or mental impairment that substantially limits an individual's major life activities. The definition also encompasses the history of an impairment and the perception of having an impairment. There are over one thousand different impairments that are covered by this act, including intellectual disabilities.

The ADA requires employers to make a "reasonable accommodation" for those applicants or employees able to perform the "essential" functions of the job with reasonable proficiency. An accommodation is considered unreasonable only in those instances where undue physical or financial hardship is placed on the employer.

Pregnancy Discrimination Act of 1978 (PDA). The PDA recognizes pregnancy as a temporary disability and prohibits sex discrimination based on pregnancy, childbirth, or related conditions. Women must be permitted to work as long as they are capable of performing the essential functions of their current job or any promotional or transfer opportunities. If an employer insists on establishing special rules for pregnancy, such rules must be dictated by business necessity or related to issues of health or safety.

Immigration Reform and Control Act of 1986 (IRCA). IRCA makes it illegal for employers to discriminate against individuals on the basis of their citizenship or national origin in all matters of employment. Employers are also prohibited from knowingly employing illegal aliens. IRCA has established requirements for employers to determine an individual's authorization to work in the United States. The act applies to employers with four or more workers. The Immigration and Naturalization Service (INS) dtermines what constitutes an acceptable document proving work eligibility and identity. A list of these documents may be obtained by visiting IRCA's home page at http://www.usda.gov/oce/oce/labor-affairs/ircasumm.htm.

Civil Rights Act of 1991. The Civil Rights Act of 1991 provides appropriate remedies for intentional discrimination and unlawful harassment in the workplace. It extends beyond the Civil Rights Act of 1964 by providing coverage to U.S. citizens employed at a U.S. company's foreign site. In addition, the burden of proof is placed on employers to show lack of discrimination.

A summary of key federal fair employment laws appears in Exhibit 3–1.

State Laws

State and local laws may differ from federal legislation and should also be considered. For example, several states make it illegal to make employment

---

xhibit 3–1

Federal Fair Employment Laws Pertaining to Performance Appraisals

- *Civil Rights Act of 1964:*
  Prohibits discrimination on the basis of race, color, religion, sex, and national origin in all matters of employment.

- *Equal Pay Act of 1963:*
  Requires equal pay for men and women performing substantially equal work.

- *Age Discrimination in Employment Act of 1967:*
  Prohibits discrimination in all matters of employment, regardless of how old the employee may be.

- *Americans with Disabilities Act of 1990:*
  Prohibits discrimination against individuals with disabilities.

- *Pregnancy Discrimination Act of 1978:*
  Women who are pregnant may not be denied equal employment opportunities; women must be permitted to work as long as they are capable of performing the essential functions of their current job or any job to which they have been promoted or transferred.

- *Immigration Reform and Control Act (IRCA) of 1986:*
  Prohibits discrimination against individuals on the basis of citizenship or national origin in all matters of employment.

- *Civil Rights Act of 1991:*
  Extends coverage afforded by the Civil Rights Act of 1964 by providing additional remedies for intentional discrimination and unlawful harassment in the workplace.

---

decisions based on AIDS/HIV status. The list includes: Alaska, Arizona, California, Colorado, Connecticut, Delaware, District of Columbia, Florida, Hawaii, Illinois, Iowa, Kansas, Kentucky, Massachusetts, Michigan, Minnesota, Missouri, Nebraska, New Jersey, New York, North Carolina, Rhode Island, Utah, Vermont, Washington, West Virginia, and Wisconsin.

Likewise, it is illegal to make employment decisions based on sexual orientation in California, District of Columbia, Hawaii, Maine, Maryland, Massachusetts, Minnesota, Nevada, New Hampshire, New Jersey, New Mexico, New York, Rhode Island, Vermont, and Wisconsin.

Some states are passing legislation concerning the illegality of using genetic testing information as part of the employment process. The list includes Arizona, Arkansas, California, Hawaii, Louisiana, Maine, Maryland, Massachusetts, Michigan, Minnesota, Missouri, Nebraska, Nevada, New Hampshire, New Jersey, New York, North Carolina, Oklahoma, Oregon, Rhode Island, South Dakota, Texas, Vermont, Virginia, Washington, and Wisconsin.

An increasing trend is for individual states to have unique categories of discrimination. For instance, New York has legislation concerning political activities, North Dakota protects those receiving public assistance, Rhode Island protects domestic abuse victims, and Washington D.C. specifically protects individuals with hepatitis C.

As with federal legislation, failure to comply with any of these state or local laws could result in costly litigation.

At-Will Relationship

Employment laws do not preclude the employment- and termination-at-will doctrines, which grant employers the right to terminate, at any time, for any reason, with or without cause, the employment of an individual who does not have a written contract defining the terms of employment, provided such termination does not violate state or federal laws. In exercising this right, employers are unlikely to incur legal liability. Likewise, employees may quit at any time for any reason, without repercussion.

That said, employees have additional rights protecting them from arbitrary acts of termination-at-will. The broadest form of protection, implied covenants of good faith and fair dealing, requires employers to prove "just cause" before terminating an employee. Public policy rights may also protect employees from being fired for exercising rights such as "whistle-blowing"—public disclosure of illegal actions taken by one's company—or for refusing to perform illegal acts on behalf of an employer.

The issue of implied contract rights may arise and erode the at-will relationship. For example, a manager may say the following to an employee during a performance appraisal meeting, or write it down on an employee's appraisal form: "Your work is outstanding. I expect to see you taking over my job when I retire in a year." This statement could be construed as an implied contract. If, when the manager retires, that employee is not promoted, the information could be used as the basis of a lawsuit alleging discrimination.

✎ Exercise: Implied Contract

Consider the following statements and determine whether they could potentially be viewed as an implied contract, thereby eroding the employer's at-will relationship with its employees. If you believe the statement is "safe," move on to the next statement. If, however, you feel there is cause for concern, that is the wording is "unsafe," amend it accordingly.

1. "Jake's performance over the past year has been exemplary. He has met, and in many instances, exceeded the requirements of the job."

   I think the language of this statement is: _____ safe _____ unsafe.

   I think the language of this statement could be considered an implied contract and should be amended as follows:

   _____

   _____

2. "Who knew when I hired you a year ago that you'd turn out to be such a superstar! Here's hoping you don't get tired of us and take your talents elsewhere!"

   I think the language of this statement is: _____ safe _____ unsafe.

   I think the language of this statement could be considered an implied contract and should be amended as follows:

   _____

   _____

3. "Chris, I know you've heard some talk about reductions in staff. I just want to assure you that as long as I have anything to say about it, your job is secure."

   I think the language of this statement is: _____ safe _____ unsafe.

   I think the language of this statement could be considered an implied contract and should be amended as follows:

   _____

   _____

4. "I want you to know that I plan on recommending you for a promotion to senior analyst; that is, of course, assuming your work continues to be as excellent as it has been to date."

   I think the language of this statement is: _____ safe _____ unsafe.

   I think the language of this statement could be considered an implied contract and should be amended as follows:

   _____

   _____

HINTS, SUGGESTIONS, AND SOME ANSWERS

1. "Jake's performance over the past year has been exemplary. He has met, and in many instances, exceeded the requirements of the job."
   I think the language of this statement is: X safe _____ unsafe.

2. "Who knew when I hired you a year ago that you'd turn out to be such a superstar! Here's hoping you don't get tired of us and take your talents elsewhere!"
   I think the language of this statement is: _____ safe ___X___ unsafe.
   I think the language of this statement could be considered an implied contract and should be amended as follows: *Your performance thus far has been outstanding.*"

3. "Chris, I know you've heard some talk about reductions in staff. I just want to assure you that as long as I have anything to say about it, your job is secure."
   I think the language of this statement is: _____ safe ___X___ unsafe.
   I think the language of this statement could be considered an implied contract and should be amended as follows: *"Chris, I know you've heard some talk about reductions in staff. I'll be sure to let you know as soon as I learn anything concrete."*

4. "I want you to know that I plan on recommending you for a promotion to senior analyst; that is, of course, assuming your work continues to be as excellent as it has been to date."
   I think the language of this statement is: _____ safe ___X___ unsafe.
   I think the language of this statement could be considered an implied contract and should be amended as follows: *"Your work as an analyst has been excellent. I'd like to hear about your about your future aspirations and career goals."*

The easiest way to avoid at-will conflicts during the performance appraisal process is to focus on how the employee has performed in the past. That is not to say that you should not work with the employee to set goals, but do not make commitments connected with those goals. Also, steer clear of phrases such as, "We treat employees like members of our family," thereby suggesting job security. In addition, declare in writing, that all dealings between employer and employees are of an at-will nature and do not constitute an employment contract or a guarantee of employment.

Because the legal issues involving employment and termination-at-will are still evolving, employers are advised to have all written materials pertaining to the employment process reviewed by counsel.

Performance Appraisals and Terminations

See if you can relate to this scenario: As the manager of a fast-paced department Jeff strives to ensure a harmonious environment for his workers. For the most part, everyone gets along with the exception of Sean, who seems to thrive on being disruptive. While he always gets his work in on time, he annoys his colleagues to the point where they are often late handing in their assignments. He is frequently described as a "gnat," in that he hovers around the desks of the other workers, moving papers and other items around on their desks while talking nonstop about trivial matters. Whenever Jeff has spoken to him about his behavior he has been cordial and assured Jeff that he would be more sensitive to his coworkers' feelings.

One day one of Jeff's best workers resigns, saying she has had it with Sean; she just can no longer concentrate. Jeff is furious, thinking Sean is the one who should resign. There is only one thing left to do. Jeff seeks him out and says, "Sean, enough is enough! You're fired!" Jeff is confident, based on Sean's track record, that he will have no trouble upholding Sean's termination if challenged.

Jeff may be in for a surprise. When he informs HR of his action, he is met with a frown. It appears that all of Jeff's past written performance appraisals of Sean were glowing, rating his work in all but one category as outstanding. When it came to "ability to work with others," Jeff had rated Sean as "good," without any supporting information. In addition, there were no memos in Sean's file referencing conversations with Jeff about his behavior. To an objective onlooker, Sean appeared to be an ideal employee, and the matter seemed ripe for a charge of wrongful termination.

No one is saying Jeff should not have taken measures, perhaps including termination, to change Sean's disruptive ways. What Jeff failed to do, however, was to link Sean's past performance appraisals with his termination. In other words, the performance appraisals did not support Sean's termination.

The message here is clear: despite protection offered by employment- and termination-at-will, every employer is at risk of being sued if it does not make a connection between performance appraisals with termination. If an employee's performance deteriorates after a formal review, then subsequent documentation should support termination. (This will be discussed later in this chapter.)

Legal and Job-Specific Language

I once attended a workshop conducted by an attorney entitled, "How to Write a Performance Appraisal." I noted, with surprise, that the session was scheduled to run less than an hour. Forty-five minutes later I understood why. The attorney made clear that he had seen so many performance appraisals containing inappropriate and illegal language resulting in lawsuits that he was now advising managers to limit themselves to a handful of benign phrases. As I recall, two of his favorite "safe" phrases were, "Employee meets the requirements of the job," and "Employee's job performance is consistent with the requirements of the job." When it came to specific job responsibilities, he recommended referencing language lifted directly from the job description and having it reviewed by an attorney. For example, "This job requires interacting with senior management at monthly sales meetings; employee performs this job function in an acceptable manner."

While it was difficult to argue with the logic of his recommendation, I also found it to be somewhat sterile and safe to a fault. The statements would hold up in court, but they were otherwise ineffective and uninformative. They also failed to speak to specific job tasks.

There is a way to construct statements so that they are both legal and job-specific. Let's look at two examples:

1. This job requires the ability to create ad campaigns consistent with our clients' objectives. Regina has received letters of appreciation for her ad campaigns from three out of four of our top clients. Her work in this area is outstanding.
2. Administrative assistants are expected to help support the work of other departments, as needed. Jonah's performance in this regard is erratic and thus earns him a rating of "average."

Both of these statements begin with a reference to a specific aspect of the job, followed by an objective evaluation.

✎ Exercise: Legal and Job-Specific Language

Assume that Larry is a sales representative with a monthly goal of bringing in five new accounts. Based on this information, rewrite the following statement so that it is both legal and job-specific: "Larry needs to work harder at bringing in new accounts."

_____

_____

HINTS, SUGGESTIONS, AND SOME ANSWERS

"Larry is currently averaging four new accounts each month. The goal we jointly agreed upon is five. Larry needs to explore various avenues and utilize different resources so that he can achieve that goal."

METHODS OF APPRAISAL

While human resources professionals are generally responsible for the implementation of their organization's performance appraisal process, managers are increasingly being asked for their input when it comes to selecting the most suitable method. After all, it is the managers who complete the written review and discuss the contents with their employees; it stands to reason, therefore, that they have some say as to the appraisal system selected for use. Of course, senior management also needs to be on board with whatever method is selected.

The challenge of selecting a specific method that best meets the needs of a specific organization's employees and receives the approval of HR, managers, and senior management need not be overwhelming if one first focuses on identifying those criteria common to all appraisal methods.

Think About It...

Would you define your organization's current appraisal method as

. . . easy for managers to implement? _____ yes _____ no
. . . easy for employees to understand? _____ yes _____ no
. . . useful in making promotional decisions? _____ yes _____ no
. . . useful in making salary decisions? _____ yes _____ no
. . . relevant to employee development? _____ yes _____ no

Common Criteria

Before selecting an appraisal method for your organization, consider the five criteria that all approaches have in common:

1. *Ease of implementation by managers.* Appraisal methods should be easy for managers to navigate, complete, and communicate. Categories for completion should be clearly delineated and all terms should be succinctly defined.
2. *Ease of comprehension by employees.* Employees should have no trouble understanding the categories of evaluation, the language used to define each category, or their corresponding ratings. Differences between ratings should be distinct.
3. *Usefulness in making promotion decisions.* The categories of individual ratings and then the cumulative rating should lend themselves to comments that make clear to anyone reading the appraisal whether the employee qualifies for promotion.
4. *Usefulness in making salary decisions.* As with usefulness in making promotional decisions, the categories of an appraisal method should lend themselves to drawing a logical conclusion about changes in salary.
5. *Relevance to employee development.* Appraisal methods should focus not only on a review of past performance and success in meeting previously determined goals, but look ahead to future goals and employee development.

Choosing the Most Suitable Appraisal Method

Once you have become familiar with the five criteria common to all appraisal methods, you can identify the one that best meets the needs of your organization. Workplace particulars, such as the size of your organization as well as varying job classifications, will influence relevance for use.

Here are five popular appraisal methods:

1. *Management by Objectives (MBO).* Developed by Peter Drucker many years ago, MBO continues to be one of the most widely used appraisal methods, especially with exempt level employees. Each employee is appraised according to his or her ability to achieve mutually agreed-upon objectives.

Generally, the objectives are stated in quantitative terms, such as increasing sales by a certain percentage within a set time.

2. *Graphic Rating Scale.* The graphic rating scale lists various work factors, such as quality of work, job knowledge, and attendance. Accompanying this list of factors is a series of boxes that the evaluator checks off, each with a descriptive word generally ranging from "outstanding" to "unsatisfactory" (or some variations thereof). Sometimes a point value is assigned to each of these words. Finally, there is an overall summary rating at the end in descriptive terms and possibly point form.

3. *Behaviorally Anchored Rating Scale (BARS).* BARS is based on the characteristics of a specific job or job family. The primary duties and responsibilities of a job are identified on a form, as well as the most and least effective ways for accomplishing these functions. The manager then matches the employee's behavior with the most accurate descriptions.

4. *Forced Distribution.* Forced distribution is similar to grading on a curve. Managers are asked to rate employees on the basis of percentage categories: for example, the top ten percent of the group, the next twenty percent, the middle forty percent, the next twenty percent, and the bottom ten percent.

5. *360-Degree Evaluation.* With the 360-degree method of appraisal, performance input is received from several sources in addition to the manager. Employees may be rated by their peers, direct reports, clients, customers, and outside vendors, according to predetermined job-specific competencies. Raters generally remain anonymous to provide a well-rounded evaluation. Additional information on the 360-degree evaluation method appears in Chapter 4.

Self-Evaluation

Increasingly, employers are asking employees to conduct self-evaluations to supplement their organization's formal method of appraisal. Indeed, self-evaluation may be part of the 360-degree method of appraisal. This allows employees to compare their own assessments with those of their managers,

Think About It...

Suppose you were asked to conduct a self-evaluation and described yourself as highly motivated and responsive to simultaneously handling multiple tasks; your manager, however, finds you to be reticent and somewhat linear in your approach to completing assignments. How would you react?

Do you think your reaction would be any different had you not be asked to conduct a self-evaluation? _____ yes _____ no. Why?

and vice versa. Employees may be asked to complete the same appraisal form as their manager, or to respond to isolated categories such as: perceived strengths and areas requiring improvement; areas in which greater experience and/or education is desired; aspects of their work environment that they find helpful; changes in their work environment that would help improve performance; aspects of their work that they enjoy and, conversely, dislike; projects or tasks they would like to work on; immediate career goals; long-term career plans; and steps needed to achieve immediate and long-term goals.

Self-evaluation can enhance employer-employee relations if both parties remain open-minded and receptive to differing views. Additional information concerning self-evaluation appears in Chapter 4.

POSITION DESCRIPTIONS

It is impossible to determine whether an employee is doing an effective job without something tangible against which to measure his or her performance. Therefore, before conducting appraisals, employers need to identify the qualifications needed to do a job, as well as to clearly state the specific tasks employees are expected to perform. This is best accomplished in the form of a position description.

Position descriptions have two primary purposes: to identify the essential functions of a job, and to clarify what the incumbent is expected to accomplish. Position descriptions form the groundwork for an agreement between an employer and the incumbent regarding expected job performance results.

Job Requirements

Job requirements are position-specific educational and prior experience prerequisites. In other words, they are a way of identifying the skills and knowledge needed to successfully perform the primary duties and responsibilities of a job.

All educational and prior experience requirements should accurately and realistically reflect the level and nature of the position. In addition, said requirements should be able to stand up under legal scrutiny.

Education
Requiring a college degree or even a high school diploma may get you into legal trouble if you cannot show that someone without the degree or diploma could successfully perform the essential functions of a job. In addition, an educational prerequisite may produce a person who attended and graduated from school, but it does not, in and of itself, reflect what that person learned or is capable of doing. On the other hand, job-related educational accomplishments can speak volumes about a person's qualifications.

Carefully worded terminology with regard to educational requirements will allow latitude in making a selection. Examples include: "degree in

_____ highly desired"; "degree in _____ preferred"; and "advanced degree a plus." By using broad language, employers can select someone with extensive educational credentials if they wish, but they can also choose someone who meets the minimum requirements of the job. Terminology such as "an equivalent combination of education and experience" is also desirable, in that it is unlikely to violate any employment laws.

Experience

Prior experience requirements are stated in both tangible and intangible terms. Examples of tangible experience requirements include: "demonstrated ability to lift cartons weighing 20–40 pounds", "proven track record of increasing sales monthly", and "substantial experience in preparing annual budget reports." Examples of intangible experience requirements include: "evidence of ability to establish and maintain rapport with coworkers", "proven ability to successfully communicate with attendees of training programs", and "demonstrated skill in negotiating."

Duties and Responsibilities

Position descriptions typically list duties and responsibilities in a logical, sequential order, beginning with the task requiring the greatest amount of time or carrying the most responsibility. Action words are used to help convey to the reader a degree of responsibility. For example, compare "directs" to "under the direction of."

Maximum effectiveness can be achieved if the language conveys the purpose behind the task. Compare the following statements:

Statement A: "Maintains data on departmental transactions; prepares reports as needed."

Statement B: "Maintains data on departmental transactions concerning the projected expansion; prepares and submits reports needed for long-term organizational forecasting to members of senior management."

Statement A reflects language from a standard list-approach to writing position descriptions. It is accurate and descriptive, and uses action words ("maintains" and "prepares"); however, it is incomplete in that it fails to clarify what the incumbent is expected to accomplish. When it comes time to conduct a performance appraisal, *Statement B* better defines the task and the purpose behind it, thereby allowing for an evaluation of how successful the employee has been in performing that specific task.

✎ Exercise: Duties and Responsibilities

Expand on the following statement by converting it into one that better defines the task and the purpose behind it. The framework for the revised version is offered on the next page.

Greets visitors and determines where they need to go.

Assists visitors by _____ and _____.

HINTS, SUGGESTIONS, AND SOME ANSWERS

Assists visitors by welcoming them to Vixter, Inc., ascertaining their desired location, *and* providing them with directions.

DISCIPLINARY ACTION AND DOCUMENTATION

Not every employee is entitled to receive a glowing performance appraisal. Since most reviews are conducted annually, it is not unrealistic to presume that, at some point during the year, some employees will experience performance-related problems. Yet, HR professionals who have received hundreds of performance appraisals prepared by managers will attest that one would never think this was the case in that so many employees are rated as "outstanding." This occurs because managers typically fail to take disciplinary action when it is warranted, are uneasy about documenting any disciplinary action that is taken, or do not reference any action taken in the written appraisal or face-to-face appraisal meeting. When asked why they do not evaluate poor performers candidly, managers invariably, and somewhat sheepishly, reply with one of three reasons: (1) to avoid a potentially disagreeable confrontation, (2) to hope that the employee knows he/she needs to improve and will be motivated to do so on his/her own, or (3) to hope the employee will opt for a transfer or quit. Rarely do employees set about developing a plan for improved performance on their own; even more unusual are those employees who decide to leave because of their sub-par performance. Instead, the situation continues, often becoming worse, until managers reach a breaking point.

It does not have to be this way. Performance appraisals that are predicated on job-related issues legitimately calling for disciplinary action and documentation provide managers with an effective and painless tool for accurately identifying less-than-ideal employee performance.

PROGRESSIVE DISCIPLINARY STEPS

Most of the time if managers are doing their jobs as coaches as counselors (Chapter 2), disciplinary action can be avoided. Sometimes, however, despite a manager's best efforts, counseling is ineffective and ends up serving as prelude to progressive disciplinary action.

The purpose of progressive discipline is to make a last attempt to motivate employees toward resolving performance-related issues in a constructive and productive manner. If the employee fails to respond, then formal steps should be taken that may possibly end in termination.

The following steps are intended as a guide in most types of infractions, such as excessive tardiness or absenteeism. Certain serious occurrences, such as acts of physical violence, may warrant suspension or immediate dismissal. For general disciplinary guidelines, see Exhibit 3–2.

xhibit 3–2
General Disciplinary Guidelines

- Gather and objectively evaluate all the facts before deciding on a course of action.
- Administer discipline at the time an infraction occurs.
- Correlate the degree of discipline with the seriousness of the offense, the frequency of its occurrence, its effect on productivity and other employees, and the employee's overall employment history.
- Discipline employees for violating rules with which they are familiar.
- Apply disciplinary procedures uniformly and consistently.
- Apply the sequence of disciplinary steps for a repeat of the same infraction.
- Administer discipline in private.

Step 1: Verbal warning. Verbal warnings should build on prior attempts at counseling and serve as a final attempt to clarify misunderstood directions, eliminate incorrect assumptions, and resolve any conflicts.

Step 2: First written warning. A written warning is issued if the same problem recurs despite a verbal warning. This is a brief statement of what happened, who was involved, when and where the unacceptable behavior took place, why it warrants a written warning, and what improvement is expected. The employee should be given an opportunity to read the statement and make comments, both verbally and in writing. He or she should then be asked to sign the written warning, indicating understanding of its contents.

Step 3: Second written warning. If the problem persists or is repeated, it may result in a second written warning. Should this occur, the guidelines described under Step 2 should be applied.

Step 4: Suspension. If the problem continues, suspension may be warranted. Suspensions are usually for a period of one to three working days, with or without pay. Employers that suspend with pay treat the act more as a leave whereby the employee is expected to reflect on his or her transgressions and additionally appreciate the organization's good-faith effort to convert wrongdoings into productive behavior. Employers that suspend without pay feel the act is severe and, as such, the employee should not be rewarded.

Whether the suspension is with or without pay, the employee should be told of the reasons for the suspension, and warned that failure to improve in work or conduct could result in termination.

Step 5: Termination. After a verbal warning, two written warnings, and suspension, termination for repeated or continued infractions may be called for. A written statement summarizing the reasons for termination should be placed in the employee's HR file.

PERFORMANCE APPRAISAL FORMS

Throughout my years in human resources, I have seen performance appraisal forms ranging from essays to reliance on numerical ratings. There

Think About It...

What do you project to be the likely outcome for an employee who demonstrates chronic tardiness in an organization that lacks progressive disciplinary steps?

_____

_____

Contrast your projected outcome with that of an employee who demonstrates chronic tardiness in an organization that has the progressive five disciplinary steps identified on the previous page.

_____

_____

have been forms with irrelevant categories, unclear or insufficient instructions, and a minimal amount of space for employee comments. Some try to cover too much; others err on the side of extreme brevity. I have also seen forms used as substitutes for face-to-face discussions between managers and employees, or used to address non-job-related issues. And of course, there are some organizations that avoid forms all together.

The primary purpose of performance appraisal forms should be to facilitate the face-to-face meeting between the appraising manager and the employee being reviewed. As such, when used effectively, forms can provide invaluable support to the performance appraisal process.

Ways in Which Appraisal Forms Are Effectively Used

Performance appraisal forms are maximally effective when they are used to accomplish ten key objectives:

1. To highlight an employee's performance from the last review, or date of hire, to the present, in relation to the job requirements and responsibilities identified in the position description
2. To identify strengths and areas requiring improvement
3. To develop a career development plan, enabling the employee to build on his or her strengths
4. To develop an action plan, including methods and a timetable for improvement
5. To establish job-specific goals to be met by the time of the next formal performance appraisal
6. To make decisions about salary increases, promotions, transfers, demotions, and terminations
7. To help human resources ensure relevance between appraisal conclusions and recommendations about salary increases, promotions, transfers, demotions, and terminations
8. To help resolve disciplinary matters

9. To document the need for training
10. To allow employees the opportunity to openly express their views about a manager's assessment

Well-designed forms can help employers achieve these objectives, while poorly designed or misused forms can render the system virtually useless. For this reason, using another organization's form for your own is not recommended, no matter how similar the other organization may be in composition, size, goals, and so on. Your form should reflect your organization's unique work environment.

Ways in Which Appraisal Forms Are Ineffectively Used

Just as there are ways to enhance the use of performance appraisal forms, so too are there ways to render them ineffective. Here are five of the most common misuses of performance appraisal forms:

1. *Complete and submit the appraisal form to HR without first discussing the contents with the employee.* This translates into a lost opportunity for the employee to discuss the various categories being evaluated or to review means for improving performance. It also precludes the opportunity for managers and employees to set performance objectives together for the next review period.
2. *Meet with an employee to discuss performance prior to completing the form.* The manager may use the blank form as a guide for the meeting, reviewing the various categories and commenting verbally on the employee's performance in each, but without anything written down.
3. *Complete the form and submit it to the employee for review, comment, and signature.* This negates any face-to-face discussion, a vital part of the appraisal process. Face-to-face interaction between the employee and the manager is essential for maintaining a positive working relationship, planning objectives for the next review period, and encouraging career development.
4. *Change comments on the form after meeting face-to-face with the employee.* These changes are often negative, and typically occur when then employee says something during the interview that makes the appraiser thinks he or she was too generous with the original rating. Sometimes, however, managers are convinced by employees that they were originally too harsh, and upgrade the ratings accordingly.
5. *Relying too much on numerical ratings.* This commonly occurs because numerical ratings are so easy to use; however, it is this very ease of use that renders them ineffective when they stand alone. That is, terms accompanying the numbers rarely provide an adequate portrayal of an employee's performance. Accordingly, if your form uses numerical ratings it should also provide space for supportive statements.

Rating Terminology

A stumbling block for many organizations is the rating terminology used on a performance appraisal form. There is not only a wide range of language from which to choose, but one must also typically select from three to five groups of terms. Each grouping has advantages and disadvantages.

Five Grouping Terms

Here are some examples of five grouping terms:

- *Far exceeds* the requirements of the job, *exceeds* the requirements of the job, *meets* the requirements of the job, *occasionally meets* the requirements of the job, *fails to meet* the requirements of the job
- *Always meets* the requirements of the job, *consistently meets* the requirements of the job, *often* meets the requirements of the job, *sometimes meets* the requirements of the job, *rarely meets* the requirements of the job
- *Invariably meets* the requirements of the job, *regularly meets* the requirements of the job, *usually meets* the requirements of the job, *occasionally meets* the requirements of the job, *never meets* the requirements of the job

Five grouping terms are the most popular. Managers report that they feel they can make a more accurate selection from among five statements. On the other hand, with five choices comes the inevitable middle-of-the-road term, which, regardless of the actual term used, is translated into "average." For managers who are uneasy about providing criticism or praise, this is an easy route to follow. To prevent this from happening, some organizations design their five-term forms so that the order is switched around for each competency being rated. It has the effect of a speed bump, in that the appraiser has to slow down and read each statement to ensure they are checking off the right one. This technique is designed to encourage managers to put some thought into selecting the statement that best reflects the employee's work, while backing it up with specific examples.

Four Grouping Terms

Consider some popular four grouping terms:

- *Superior* performance, *commendable* performance, *acceptable* performance, *unacceptable* performance
- *Extraordinary* work, *excellent* work, *good* work, *poor* work

---

?   **Think About It...**

Put a check mark next the terminology grouping you prefer:

_____ three-term grouping _____ four-term grouping _____ five-term grouping

Give a reason for your selection:

_____

_____

_____

- *Outstanding ability* meet job expectations, *very good ability* to meet job expectations, *fair ability* to meet job expectations, *poor ability* to meet job expectations

Four grouping terms are desirable in that they do not suffer from that middle rating syndrome associated with five grouping terms. However, having four choices can compel appraisers to select from what is perceived as either the positive or negative side.

Three Grouping Terms

Some employers opt for three grouping terms, believing it makes an appraiser's job easier:

- *Above* average performance, *average* performance, *below* average performance
- *Exceeds* expectations, *meets* expectations, *fails* to meet expectations
- *Exceptional* work, *acceptable* work, *unacceptable* work

Three grouping terms are, by their very nature, limiting. They also present the same dilemma as five grouping terms, in that there is a middle "average" choice. On the other hand, some managers say they like three choices because they find it easier to select from among three broad terms.

The most effective way to avoid problems associated with each of these methods is to require supporting statements or examples to accompany each rating. That way, regardless of whether a five-, four-, or three-term rating is chosen, there is rationale for the appraiser's selection. In addition, providing definitions of what each term means directly on the form will help managers gauge the appropriate term to select.

Despite the fact that managers are not legal experts, they still must be familiar with the legal side of performance appraisals. This includes an understanding of relevant fair employment laws on both a federal and state level, familiarity with the at-will relationship between employers and employees, awareness of the legal connection between performance appraisals and terminations, and knowledge of legal and job specific language.

While human resources professionals are generally responsible for the implementation of their organization's performance appraisal process, managers are increasingly being asked for their input when it comes to selecting the most suitable method. In making a selection, managers need to factor in those criteria common to all appraisal methods: difficulty of implementation by managers, difficulty of comprehension by employees, usefulness in making promotional decisions, usefulness in making salary decisions and relevance to employee development. Typically, one of five popular methods is selected: management by objectives, graphic rating scale, behaviorally anchored rating scale, forced distribution, or 360-degree evaluation. Many organizations also ask employees to conduct self-evaluations.

Before conducting appraisals, employers need to identify the qualifications needed to do a job, and clearly state the specific tasks employees are expected to perform. This is best accomplished in the form of a position description.

Not every employee should receive the highest rating possible on his or her performance appraisal. Yet, this often occurs either because a manager fails to take and document disciplinary action when it is warranted, is uneasy about documenting any disciplinary action that is taken, or does not reference any action taken in the written appraisal or face-to-face meeting. Progressive disciplinary steps can help guide managers and better prepare them when it comes time to conduct the formal performance appraisal.

Performance appraisal forms should be used to facilitate the face-to-face meeting between the appraising manager and the employee being reviewed. Carefully selected rating terminology supported by examples will render the forms maximally effective.

Review Questions

1. Position descriptions have two primary purposes: one is to identify the essential functions of a job, the other is to:
   (a) tell the employee how to perform a given job.
   (b) clarify what the incumbent is expected to accomplish.
   (c) describe the performance of the ideal employee in a given job.
   (d) list all tasks expected of the incumbent.

1. (b)

2. The easiest way to avoid at-will conflicts during the performance appraisal process is to:
   (a) avoid setting goals.
   (b) avoid putting anything in writing.
   (c) focus on how the employee has performed in the past.
   (d) have the employee sign a statement absolving you from any wrongdoing.

2. (c)

3. Performance appraisal forms are maximally effective when they are used to accomplish ten key objectives. One of these is to:
   (a) identify strengths and areas requiring improvement.
   (b) meet with an employee to discuss performance prior to completing the form.
   (c) rely on numerical ratings.
   (d) submit the completed form to the employee for review, comment, and signature.

3. (a)

4. The purpose of asking employees to conduct self-appraisals is to:
   (a) ensure agreement with the manager's appraisal.
   (b) allow employees to compare their own assessments with those of their managers, and vice versa.
   (c) minimize any chance that the employee will file a grievance if he or she disagrees with the manager's appraisal.
   (d) present a unified review to human resources.

4. (b)

Do you have questions? Comments? Need clarification?
Call Educational Services at 1-800-225-3215, ext. 600,
or email at ed_svcs@amanet.org.

5. The purpose of progressive discipline is to:
    (a) justify termination.
    (b) make clear to the employee that their behavior is unacceptable and will not be tolerated.
    (c) set an example for other employees.
    (d) make a last attempt to motivate employees toward resolving performance-related issues in a constructive, productive manner.

5. (d)

4

Preparing for Performance Appraisal Meetings

focus

Learning Objectives

By the end of this chapter, you should be able to:

- Articulate questions managers should ask themselves prior to meeting with an employee to discuss the formal performance appraisal.
- Determine the rationale for and approach to asking employees to prepare self-evaluations.
- Cull information on which the appraisal will be based.
- Anticipate possible employee reactions to their formal performance appraisal.
- Create an appropriate setting for the face-to-face appraisal meeting.

According to his boss, colleagues, and employees, Daniel was a great manager. If asked, he would modestly agree with this characterization, except for one area: conducting performance appraisals. He never objected to filling out the appraisal form; he just disliked sitting across from an employee telling them that their work was anything less than outstanding.

Daniel traced his discomfort with conducting reviews to a performance appraisal meeting with an employee who had a chronic tardiness problem. It was the first time he had to deal with an employee whom he had rated as "below average" in a category, but he was confident that the session would go well. He intended to help her develop a strategy for getting back on track, and assumed the employee would be receptive and cooperative, since she was otherwise an outstanding worker. He was stunned when she responded, instead, with surprise, then despair, and finally anger. How could she react this way? Surely she knew she was arriving at work late.

Now it was time to evaluate another of his workers who was below average in two categories. Daniel was apprehensive and decided to speak about it with Vanessa, the HR representative for his department. Let's read part of that conversation:

Daniel: Vanessa, I need some advice. I have a performance appraisal meeting coming up soon and I'm stressing over it.

Vanessa: What's the problem?

Daniel: This employee has a problem with meeting deadlines and prioritizing his assignments. The last time I had to talk with an employee with performance problems I wasn't prepared and botched it; can you help me?

Vanessa: I'll certainly try; when's his review due?

Daniel: I've got plenty of time—about four weeks—but I want to do this right.

Vanessa: Actually, Daniel, you've just taken the first step to a successful performance appraisal meeting: that is, preparation.

Daniel: It's good to know that I'm doing something right! What else do I need to do to ensure a productive meeting?

Vanessa: I'm going to prepare a packet for you, identifying specific questions managers should ask themselves before meeting with an employee.

Daniel: All right, I guess. O.K.—thanks!

Vanessa: Wait, there's more—actually quite a bit more. You'll want to consider asking him to conduct a self-appraisal.

Daniel: That sounds risky . . . are you sure that's a good idea?

Vanessa: Don't worry; I'll give you some guidelines for self-appraisals. I'll also identify sources of information on which the appraisal should be based.

Daniel: Like what?

Vanessa: Like the employee's job description, his work record, accomplishments, and areas requiring improvement.

Daniel: That makes sense. What else?

Vanessa: You also need to examine mutually agreed-upon performance objectives.

Daniel: That's logical, too. Is there more?

Vanessa: Yes; you'll want to gather input from others.

Daniel: I'm beginning to see why you're glad I'm starting this process a month in advance. Am I done preparing if I do all this?

Vanessa: Almost. You told me earlier that you were taken aback by that other employee's reaction to her review when you discussed her attendance record.

Daniel: Actually, I was shocked. I mean, she obviously knew she was late coming to work.

Vanessa: Many managers make the mistake of assuming they'll be able to predict how an employee is likely to react to their review. That's why it's so important to anticipate possible employee reactions.

Daniel: Please tell me that's it . . .

Vanessa: Almost. There's one more thing that will maximize your chances of being fully prepared for the face-to-face appraisal meeting: creating an appropriate environment.

Daniel: What does that mean?

Vanessa: I'll write out some easy-to-follow tips and include them in the packet of information I'm going to give to you.

Daniel: Great—but please, make it soon, O.K.? I've got just under a month to prepare and suddenly that doesn't seem like enough time!

 **Think About It...**

Does your organization

. . . encourage managers to prepare prior to conducting a performance appraisal meeting? _____ yes _____ no

Does this include

. . . asking managers to ensure they have done all they should prior to the meeting? _____ yes _____ no
. . . encouraging employee self-appraisals? _____ yes _____ no
. . . culling information upon which the appraisal will be based? _____ yes _____ no
. . . anticipating possible employee reactions? _____ yes _____ no
. . . creating an appropriate setting for the performance appraisal meeting? _____ yes _____ no

---

Questions Managers Should Ask Themselves

The preparation stage of conducting successful employee performance appraisals ideally begins a minimum of one month prior to the face-to-face session. During this time, managers should take care to ensure that their evaluations are fair and objective, particularly if the appraisal is unsatisfactory in one or more categories. The most sure-fire way of doing this is for managers to have a one-on-one question and answer conversation with themselves:

- Am I confident that the employee's skills and interests are properly aligned with the job?
- Is there enough of a match between the employee and myself with regard to important intangible factors, such as management style or personality, to ensure a productive working relationship?
- Does the employee have a clear understanding of the job duties and scope of responsibilities?
- Have I worked with the employee long enough (at least three months) to be able to effectively evaluate his or her performance?
- Have I objectively measured the employee's work record against the requirements of the job?
- Have I evaluated the employee's entire performance and not just positive or negative factors?
- Do I have some ideas as to how improvements can best be accomplished?
- Have I determined what assistance I'm prepared to provide toward improvement?
- Has the employee been provided with sufficient instructions and work tools?
- Have I encouraged the employee to ask questions or seek clarification regarding his or her work assignments?
- Have I anticipated the feelings and possible reactions of the employee?
- Have I explored my own feelings and ensured that I am approaching the meeting with a mind that is open and free of bias?
- Am I confident that nothing we discuss will come as a surprise to the employee?
- Am I prepared to listen to what the employee has to say without feeling defensive?
- Have I been available and supportive during instances when the employee has had an especially difficult assignment or challenging deadline to meet?

If the answer to any of these questions is no, an employee's unsatisfactory performance may have nothing to do with ability; it could, instead, be the product of the evaluating manager's failure to:

- Set mutually agreed-upon meaningful objectives
- Accurately measure accomplishments against agreed-upon objectives
- Examine personal attitudes that may interfere with an objective measurement of performance

This last statement may be the most difficult for managers to accept: after all, no one wants to think that they are anything other than impartial and nonjudgmental. Yet, posing this and the other questions well in advance of the appraisal meeting could make the difference between a productive and nonproductive session.

✎ Exercise: Questions Managers Should Ask Themselves

Jim has asked himself the previous questions while preparing for a performance appraisal meeting with his administrative assistant, Patrick. He acknowledges that, while Patrick is quite capable of performing his administrative assistant duties and clearly understands the scope of responsibility involved, he has indicated a strong desire to be trained as a compensation analyst. Jim confesses that he has put off discussing advancement possibilities with Patrick in part because of their conflicting work styles. Jim also admits that he could have done a better job with making himself available and supportive.

What impact do you think these factors will have on the performance appraisal meeting?

_____

_____

What do you think Jim can do at this point, four weeks prior to meeting with Patrick?

_____

_____

_____

HINTS, SUGGESTIONS, AND SOME ANSWERS

What impact do you think these factors will have on the performance appraisal meeting? Patrick could approach the performance appraisal meeting somewhat defensively, anticipating that Jim will not be as supportive and encouraging as he would like.

What do you think Jim can do at this point, four weeks prior to meeting with Patrick? Jim can think of ways in which he can make himself more available to Patrick: Perhaps they can schedule bi-weekly meetings to talk about whatever Patrick may be currently working on, or meet less formally over coffee. Jim can also look ahead to how he can be more supportive of Patrick's goals and aspirations. He can do this by preparing to discuss the position of compensation analyst; that is, he can review the job description and identify Patrick's skills and abilities, as well as those areas requiring improvement, in relation to the analyst's position. To accomplish these objectives, Jim must get past their conflicting work styles.

ASKING EMPLOYEES TO PREPARE SELF-EVALUATIONS

In Chapter 3, you read that employers are increasingly asking employees to conduct self-evaluations, thereby allowing employees to compare their own assessments with those of their managers, and vice versa. Employees may be asked to complete the same appraisal form as their manager, or to respond to isolated job-related categories. Let's take a closer look at self-appraisals as part of the preparation stage of performance appraisals.

Managers who have never asked employees to conduct self-appraisals often assume the results will be glowing, with outstanding results in every category. Interestingly, this is not what generally happens, especially when employees are asked to provide supporting statements for their evaluations. Boasting about one's accomplishments can be difficult; providing specific examples can be even more challenging. Conversely, identifying areas requiring improvement can be made a more palatable assignment if concrete illustrations are called for.

To help employees prepare effective self-evaluations, managers are advised to schedule a meeting about a month prior to the face-to-face appraisal session. The following dialogues illustrate some options as to how managers can introduce the subject of self-evaluations to employees, using an appraisal form:

Option #1: "(Name), as you probably know, your annual performance appraisal review date is next month. I'm going to be completing the appraisal form and thought you'd like to do the same (manager hands form to employee). Just rate yourself for each category and provide examples that support your ratings. Bring the completed form to our meeting and we'll compare my assessment with your self-evaluation. If you have any questions about what any of the categories mean, just call HR."

Option #2: "I'm going to be preparing for your annual appraisal meeting next month. I'd like to suggest that you prepare a self-review prior to our meeting so I can see how you view your performance in various categories. Let's go over a blank form (hands employee a copy of the form) so I can be assured that you understand what's required."

Option #3: "(Name), as you know, (company name) values employee input; this philosophy extends to performance appraisals. Here's our form: I'm going to be filling it out prior to our meeting on (date). I'd like you to do the same. You can either submit it to me prior to our meeting, or bring it with you. First, let's spend a few minutes going over the form to ensure that you understand the rating system."

Some organizations opt for a less formal approach to self-appraisals; that is, they do not require employees to complete forms. Instead, they may suggest one of the following approaches:

Option #1: "(Name), next month is your annual review. Before we meet, I'd like you to give some thought to how you think you've done over the past year. Jot down some notes about where you feel you've excelled, as well as any areas in which you feel there's room for improvement. Then when we meet, we'll compare your self-evaluation with how I've assessed your work."

Option #2: "Here are some questions I'd like you to take a look at and answer, (name). As you can see, they all have to do with your work performance over the past year. Get your answers to me about a week before we meet on (date). Don't let the questions about improvement throw you; if there are areas you think you need to work on, just say so."

Option #3: "I wanted to talk with you about your upcoming performance appraisal. I know it's still a month away, but I've already started thinking about how you've performed over the past year, and I'd like you to do the same. Here are some questions, (name), that tie in directly with the form I'll be completing. Don't be modest about your accomplishments; likewise, be frank if you see areas in which you feel you need to improve."

Note that these options all call for both areas of accomplishment and those requiring improvement.

CULLING INFORMATION UPON WHICH THE APPRAISAL WILL BE BASED

The preparation for an employee's annual performance appraisal includes drawing information from a variety of sources.

Position Descriptions

The primary source of information in the preparation of a performance appraisal is the employee's position description. As stated in Chapter 3, position descriptions have two primary purposes: to identify the essential functions of a job, and to clarify what the incumbent is expected to accomplish. It is logical, therefore, to use it as a foundation for performance, measuring what the employee has accomplished vis-à-vis what is required.

 **Think About It...**

Which approach to self-appraisal do you prefer?

_____ Asking the employee to complete the same form as the manager
_____ Asking the employee to respond to some questions about accomplishments and areas requiring improvement
_____ Asking the employee to submit his or her completed forms or responses to questions to the manager in advance of the face-to-face meeting
_____ Asking the employee to bring his or her completed forms or responses to questions to the manager to the face-to-face meeting

Explain your reasoning for your choice below.

_____

_____

_____

For each category on the appraisal form, the manager can simply refer to the position description for guidance. For example: let's assume that one of the categories on the performance appraisal form is "Decision Making." The appraising manager can now refer to the employee's position description and see that it calls for "identifying both existing and potential departmental problems, and developing steps or procedures to resolve these problems."

The appraising manager next looks at the rating choices. Let's say he or she is working with a five grouping classification of terms: *Far exceeds* the requirements of the job, *exceeds* the requirements of the job, *meets* the requirements of the job, *occasionally meets* the requirements of the job, *fails to meet* the requirements of the job. By factoring in the employee's work record, mutually agreed-upon performance objectives, and input from others (see below), the manager can determine which rating best applies. These factors will provide supporting information for the selected rating.

Employee's Work Record

Throughout the year, between formal performance appraisal reviews, managers are responsible for observing and noting employee accomplishments and areas requiring improvement.

Accomplishments

Keeping a simple log of employee accomplishments when they occur can be useful when it comes time for a formal review. Here are some examples:

- February 21, 2xxx: Amanda offered to stay late to help collate the budget for the next day's board meeting. It took an additional three hours to complete, but she never complained; in fact, she was the most cheerful person there.
- May 16, 2xxx: When Marc called in sick on the morning of our annual regional sales meeting, Amanda offered to perform his duties as well as her own to ensure that everything went smoothly. She did so and the sales meeting came off without a hitch.
- September 19, 2xxx: Amanda voluntarily covered the telephones during her lunch hour when Jessica returned late from a doctor's appointment.
- November 27, 2xxx: In response to the memo calling for one volunteer in every department to remain until 4:00PM on the day before Thanksgiving, Amanda didn't hesitate to volunteer.

These statements will serve as solid support for ratings on the performance appraisal form. If, for instance, the manager selects "Far exceeds the requirements of the job" in the category "Cooperation," Amanda's willingness to stay at work the day before a holiday, cover the telephones during lunch, perform someone else's duties in addition to her own, and stay late at work all reflect a cooperative spirit. The dated details lend far more credence that simply stating, "Amanda frequently exhibits a willingness to cooperate."

Areas Requiring Improvement

Many managers struggle with negative reviews. While it is admittedly harder to tell someone they need improvement than it is to administer praise, the task can be made more palatable if there is a documented basis for the assessment. Matters warranting both coaching and counseling (Chapter 2) lend themselves to documenting specifics about areas requiring improvement.

Let's recall an example of spontaneous coaching from Chapter 2 that may serve as a reference in the employee's annual review. Jocelyn, a customer service manager, overheard one of her representatives, Becky, speak rudely to a customer. After Jocelyn discussed the matter with Becky, she returned to her office and made this notation: "August 7, 2xxx: overheard Becky's side of a conversation with a customer. Spoke with her about her tone; that is, how important it is for customer service reps to be courteous and try to end conversations on a positive note. Becky acknowledged that she could have handled the situation in a calmer, more cooperative way, and offered to call the customer the following day to rectify the matter."

During the preparation of Becky's review, Jocelyn may choose to rate her as "usually meets the requirements of the job" when it comes to "customer relations," referencing the August 7 incident. Depending on what happens subsequent to that date, Jocelyn could write, "Since then, there have been no further incidences requiring coaching."

Mutually Agreed-Upon Performance Objectives

One of the most important aspects of an employee's initial performance appraisal meeting is establishing mutually agreed-upon performance objectives for the next review. Then, in preparation for the next session, the manager can revisit these objectives and determine how successful the employee has been in achieving them. This also sets the stage for jointly establishing objectives for the upcoming review period.

Let's consider a specific example involving Marie, a sales manager, and Josh, one of her sales representatives. Marie has previously suggested to Josh that he could increase the percentage of deals he closes by thirty percent each month and Josh agrees. Here's part of their exchange during Josh's annual review:

Marie: Josh, let's look at how successful you've been in meeting your performance objective of increasing the percentage of deals you close by thirty percent each month. I'm looking at your reports from July through November, and seeing an average increase of twenty percent.

Josh: I guess I was reaching too high.

Marie: Do you think so? Let's look at this more closely. It seems as if you concentrated almost exclusively on increasing sales in the northeast region of your territory. Why is that?

Josh: I've always had the greatest success there.

Marie: What do you think would happen if you tried to increase sales in your other regions?

Josh: I don't know; I've just never done as well in the other regions.

Marie: But you do make sales—just not as many. I wonder . . . if you increased sales in the northeast region by twenty percent and you apply the same skills to your other region . . . do you think you might be able to generate another ten percent in all the other regions combined?

Josh: I suppose I could; yes, I suppose I could.

Marie: Why don't we say your performance objective for next time is to maintain the increase in the percentage of deals in the northeast by twenty percent, and to increase the percentage of deals you close in other regions by ten percent each month.

Josh: I think that's doable.

Input from Others

An additional source of information upon which an appraisal may be based is information from others. This is generally accomplished via a 360-degree method of evaluation, mentioned in Chapter 3. With the 360-degree method of appraisal, performance input is received from several sources in addition to that of the manager. Employees may be rated by their peers, direct reports, clients, customers, and outside vendors, according to predetermined job-specific competencies. In many instances, the identities of these reviewers are kept confidential.

Consider this scenario: One month before meeting with her marketing associate, Isaac, Lorrie considers the various individuals with whom he regularly comes in contact. She narrows the field to five people whom she believes can provide input concerning Isaac's work performance: Rhonda, Isaac's coworker; Eric, the secretary in the marketing department; and representatives from three major companies Isaac services. Lorrie is interested in learning their views concerning Isaac's success in communicating information as it relates to new marketing plans. She asks each person to rate Isaac according to the organization's four grouping terms of "outstanding," "very good," "fair," and "poor," as well as providing one example to support each evaluation. Here's what she receives back from these individuals:

- From Rhonda: "I hate to admit it, but Isaac deserves a rating of "outstanding." He's constantly sharing his ideas about new marketing plans. The last one he pitched—the one involving multiple overlays—was ingenious. I don't have to tell you that; that campaign earned the company big bucks!"
- From Eric: "I'd give Isaac a "very good." He's really smart, but he talks too fast and I don't always understand what he wants me to do."

- From Client #1: "Isaac is excellent; that is to say, outstanding. He convinced me to take a risk and step outside of our usual marketing campaign; he was right on target."
- From Client #2: "Isaac is reliable and consistent. He's very, very good at what he does."
- From Client #3: "Outstanding; especially the way he presented the idea of using multiple overlays."

The information provided through this 360-degree technique helps Lorrie prepare for her evaluation of Isaac. Based on the feedback she has received, coupled with her own observations, Lorrie is comfortable giving Isaac a rating of "outstanding" when it comes to communicating information as it relates to new marketing plans.

ANTICIPATING POSSIBLE EMPLOYEE REACTIONS

An important step in the preparation stage for managers is anticipating possible employee reactions to their appraisals. While it is impossible to predict with certainty how an employee will respond, we have identified six behavior patterns that employees typically display during performance appraisal meetings. Here they are, along with recommended approaches for dealing with them, as well as potential outcomes (Exhibit 4–1):

Agreeable Reaction

The employee readily agrees with all ratings and suggestions, both positive and negative. For example, if the manager rates his ability to meet deadlines as "exceeds expectations," the employee might respond, "You'll get no argument from me there!" If the manager determines that the employee should work harder at generating new business, the employee replies, "Yes, you're absolutely right."

Encourage overly agreeable employees to discuss their self-evaluations first, point by point. Discuss their thoughts concerning career development before offering your evaluation.

This approach is likely to provide agreeable employees with the opportunity to express previously unvoiced feeling and opinions, thereby allowing

Think About It...

What should a manager do if he or she receives conflicting input from several sources?

_____

_____

_____

xhibit 4–1
Anticipating Possible Employee Reactions

Possible Reaction:	Agreeable
Approach:	Encourage employee to discuss his/her self-evaluation first
	Discuss employee's ideas concerning career development
Potential Outcome:	Employee will express unvoiced feelings and opinions
	Greater understanding of employee's interests
	Greater commitment to career goals
Possible Reaction:	Contrary
Approach:	Allow for a certain amount of disagreement
	Actively listen
	Seek clarification
Potential Outcome:	Clear the air
	Opportunity for a healthy dialogue
Possible Reaction:	Nervous
Approach:	Explain how the meeting benefits him or her
	Discuss areas with which employee is most comfortable
	Ask for employee's opinions
	Ask about areas of interest
Potential Outcome:	Calming effect on employee
	Opens future ways of communication
Possible Reaction:	Defensive
Approach:	Allow for a certain amount of disagreement
	Actively listen
	Address employee's performance; not personality
Potential Outcome:	Reduced levels of defensiveness
	Greater objectivity
Possible Reaction:	Silent
Approach:	Discuss areas with which employee is most comfortable
	Ask "fun" questions; relate answers to current job
Potential Outcome:	A dialogue
	Focus on performance
Possible Reaction:	Overconfident
Approach:	Additional, challenging responsibilities
	Present a balanced picture of strengths and areas requiring improvement
Potential Outcome:	Employees will assess own performance more realistically

managers to better understand the employee's interests. It could also ensure a greater commitment to defining and meeting specific career goals.

Contrary Reaction

Contrary or argumentative employees are likely to disagree with their over-all evaluations and/or specific ratings. Despite supporting information, they will cite evidence to show that a negative review is inaccurate; I actually had an employee who, upon receiving the highest possible rating in every cate-gory said, "That's not possible; I'm not perfect, you know!"

Managers can afford to allow for a certain amount of disagreement, as long as the dialogue remains constructive. They should also actively listen to what the employee is saying and seek clarification to help determine any hidden, underlying causes for the contrary behavior.

While it is easy to become annoyed with a contrary employee, managers can view this as an opportunity to clear the air. It may be that they are frus-trated in their current position, but have not identified what it is they would prefer doing; or perhaps they are uneasy about expressing how they feel. If the manager remains calm and reasonable, expressing interest in what the employee has to say, there is greater opportunity for a healthy dialogue.

Nervous Reaction

Some employees have difficulty expressing ideas or opinions. They are apprehensive and reluctant to open up and talk, regardless of what questions you ask or how encouraging you are.

You should begin by briefly explaining the purpose of the meeting and how it will benefit them. Initially discuss areas that the nervous employee knows best and feels most comfortable talking about. Ask for the employee's opinions regarding specific issues, and inquire about their areas of interest which should lend itself to a discussion of their performance objectives. This approach is likely to have a calming effect on the employee, thereby open-ing the way for future communication.

Defensive Reaction

Defensive employees appear to be overly concerned with self-protection and are quick to transfer blame to others. In addition, they tend to react emo-tionally to statements regarding areas requiring improvement, despite spe-cific examples.

As with contrary employees, managers can allow a certain amount of disagreement, as they actively listen to what the employee is saying to deter-mine the real issue at hand. Try hard to address the person's performance, and not his or her personality. This will allow you to remain objective and stay focused. Sustaining this approach could result in reduced levels of defensiveness and greater objectivity on the part of the employee.

Silent Reaction

Regardless of what you say or ask, the silent employee responds with simple nods or monosyllabic statements. Their failure to actively participate in their own evaluation process can be frustrating and counterproductive.

 **Think About It...**

Of the six employee reactions cited, which one makes you the most uneasy? Why?

_____ Agreeable Reaction

_____ Contrary Reaction

_____ Nervous Reaction

_____ Defensive Reaction

_____ Silent Reaction

_____ Overconfident Reaction

What steps can you take if confronted with the employee reaction that makes you the most uneasy?

Encourage these individuals to talk about areas with which they are familiar and comfortable. Ask them open-ended questions, such as "What's your idea of an ideal work environment?" or "Tell me about a perfect day at work—what do you see yourself doing?" Then relate their answers to their current jobs and ask them to identify common denominators. The goal of this approach is to encourage a dialogue and allow you to focus on their performance.

Overconfident Reaction

Overconfident employees never seem to tire of telling everyone that they are assets to the organization. They seem unaware of any deficiencies and therefore cannot acknowledge ways in which they may improve their performance. In addition, they may be highly critical of, and possibly amused by, feedback from others.

You should encourage overconfident employees to challenge themselves with additional responsibilities. Also present a balanced picture to them of their strengths and areas requiring improvement accompanied by specific, documented, supporting examples. This approach may enable over-confident employees to assess their own performance more realistically.

CREATE AN APPROPRIATE SETTING

There are three essential components for creating an appropriate setting for the performance appraisal meeting. Preparing in advance of the meeting to ensure suitable conditions will maximize the effectiveness of any session, especially those in which areas requiring improvement are likely to be emphasized.

Privacy

I am constantly amazed by where managers conduct performance appraisals. Some of the most memorable are: at the company's Fourth of July picnic, during lunch in the employee cafeteria, at the airport while waiting to board a plane on to a business trip. Privacy clearly was not a priority for these appraising managers! One cannot help but wonder how they would feel if their performance review were conducted in the middle of a crowd.

Privacy is an absolute requirement if employees are expected to talk freely. They must believe that what they are saying is confidential and cannot be overheard by others. This is particularly important when sensitive matters are being discussed, such as repeated and unresolved performance problems.

Some appraising managers believe a neutral location is preferable, negating any possible distractions resulting from personal items on desks or suggesting that one or the other has a "home court advantage." In truth, any private location will suffice: the manager's or the employee's office, assuming these are "real" offices with walls and doors, and not cubicles; a conference room, a borrowed office, or any other enclosed space within the company environment.

Minimum Number of Distractions

A friend of mine confided what happened when she was scheduled for her annual performance appraisal at her first job. She arrived at the appointed time, entered her boss's office and sat down. He greeted her, ceremoniously rose from his chair, came around his desk, and closed the door. He then began talking about her work. Within minutes, there was a knock on his door: "I'm sorry to bother you," said his secretary, "but Mr. Reynolds is here and just needs a minute of your time." Her boss did not hesitate: "Sure, tell him to come in." Their conversation indeed lasted only a few minutes and the meeting between my friend and her boss continued. But then the telephone rang and he answered it. This was followed by another knock on the door. The worst offense according to my friend was when she asked him a question and he did not reply initially; when he finally did he started with, "Sorry, I was just thinking about all the work I have to do!" That just about says it all!

Comfortable

If the employee is comfortable, the appraising manager will be assured of a more productive meeting. The manager's behavior and general approach to the meeting will also set the stage and often determine the comfort level of the employee. If he or she comes across as friendly, appears genuinely interested in what the employee has to say, and has made an effort to ensure privacy and prevent interruptions, then the surroundings are not going to matter a great deal.

The preparation stage of conducting successful employee performance appraisals ideally begins a minimum of one month prior to the face-to-face meeting. During this time, managers should take care to ensure that their evaluations are fair and objective, particularly if the appraisal is unsatisfactory in one or more categories. To accomplish this, managers should ask themselves a series of questions, such as "Have I worked with the employee long enough to be able to effectively evaluate his or her performance?" "Have I objectively measured the employee's work record against the requirements of the job?" and "Have I been available and supportive during instances when the employee has had an especially difficult assignment or challenging deadline to meet?" If the answer to any of these and other questions is "no," an employee's unsatisfactory performance may have nothing to do with ability.

The preparation stage continues with managers asking employees to conduct self-evaluations. Employees may be asked to complete the same appraisal form as their manager, or to respond to isolated job-related categories. This allows employees to compare their own assessments with those of their managers, and vice versa.

The primary source of information in the preparation of a performance appraisal is the employee's position description. This important document serves as a foundation for performance, measuring what the employee has accomplished vis-à-vis what is required.

The employee's work record, reflecting accomplishments and areas requiring improvement, is also used as a source of information in the preparation of performance appraisals. Keeping a simple log of events as they occur can be useful when it comes time for the employee's formal review.

One of the most important aspects of an employee's initial performance appraisal meeting is establishing mutually agreed upon performance objectives for the next review. Then, in preparation for the next session, the manager can revisit these objectives and determine how successful the employee has been in achieving them. This also sets the stage for jointly establishing objectives for the upcoming review period.

An additional source of information upon which an appraisal may be based is information from others. This is generally accomplished via a 360-degree method of evaluation, whereby input is received from several sources in addition to the manager.

Another important step in the preparation stage is for managers to anticipate possible employee reactions to their appraisal. Typically, employees react in one of six ways to performance appraisals: agreeable, contrary, nervous, defensive, silent, or overconfident.

There are three essential ingredients to creating an appropriate setting for the performance appraisal meeting: privacy, a minimum number of distractions, and comfort. Preparing in advance of the meeting to ensure suitable conditions will maximize the effectiveness of any session, especially those in which areas requiring improvements are likely to be emphasized.

Review Questions

1. To help employees prepare effective self-evaluations, managers are advised to:
   (a) ask employees to avoid writing any positive comments.
   (b) assure them that nothing they write will be used against them.
   (c) ask for ratings only, without supporting comments.
   (d) schedule a meeting about a month prior to the face-to-face appraisal meeting.

   1. (d)

2. The three essential components for creating an appropriate setting for the performance appraisal meeting are:
   (a) privacy, a minimum number of interruptions, and comfort.
   (b) an easy way out, in case the employee becomes hostile, witnesses, and comfort.
   (c) comfort, a tape recorder, and neutral territory.
   (d) privacy, a minimum number of interruptions, and a set amount of time for the meeting.

   2. (a)

3. An employee's unsatisfactory performance may have nothing to do with ability; it could, instead, be the product of the evaluating manager's failure to:
   (a) give the employee the raise he or she expected.
   (b) promote the employee.
   (c) be an effective role model.
   (d) accurately measure accomplishments against agreed-upon objectives.

   3. (d)

4. Preparing for an employee's annual performance appraisal includes drawing information from a variety of sources. This includes position descriptions, the employee's work record, mutually agreed-upon performance objectives, and:
   (a) information in their HR file.
   (b) input from others.
   (c) last year's performance appraisal.
   (d) recommendations from employees themselves.

   4. (b)

Do you have questions? Comments? Need clarification?
Call Educational Services at 1-800-225-3215, ext. 600,
or email at ed_svcs@amanet.org.

5. Employees typically display one of six behavior patterns during performance appraisal meetings. For those employees who are overly defensive, the recommended approach is to:
   (a) allow them to vent until they have nothing more to say.
   (b) let the employee know their behavior is unacceptable and that any raise they may have gotten is in serious jeopardy.
   (c) focus on the person's performance, not his or her personality.
   (d) reschedule the meeting.

5. (c)

The Written Evaluation

focus

Learning Objectives

By the end of this chapter, you should be able to:

- Explain why written performance appraisals are so important.
- Explain why writing performance appraisals are a useful tool for maximizing effective employer-employee relations.
- Describe the importance of establishing a format.
- Identify key writing dos and don'ts.
- Select appropriate language.

Very good managers often write extremely bad performance appraisals. Here is an example, taken from a written review prepared by Rob who is an intelligent, well-respected manager working for a *Fortune* 500 company. When asked how he would rate his review, he responded, "Overall, I'd say it's very good: succinct and to the point."

Here is Rob's review in its entirety. See what you think:

Job Title: Marketing Assistant

Factor: Quality of Work	*Comment:* Excellent
Factor: Productivity	*Comment:* Great job last Friday!
Factor: Job Knowledge	*Comment:* Knows his stuff
Factor: Reliability	*Comment:* Very good with paperwork
Factor: Attendance	*Comment:* Fine
Factor: Independence	*Comment:* Very good
Factor: Creativity	*Comment:* Could come up with more ideas

Factor: Decision making   *Comment:* Good
Factor: Cooperation   *Comment:* Needs to work on it
Overall rating: Mostly very good

The brevity of Rob's words, poor language selection, reference to recent events, and failure to establish a format all reflect his lack of understanding as to why written performance appraisals are important, as well as what skills are required to perform this critical task successfully.

Not surprisingly, Rob confided that he is uncomfortable writing performance appraisals, although he could not articulate why. "I just don't like doing them," was his response when asked. He added that he does not have an aversion to writing as such. He can write memos or reports of any type or length; he just dislikes writing employee reviews, whether positive or negative.

Rob is not alone in his feelings about writing employee reviews. Many otherwise effective managers are uneasy about writing performance appraisals. Why this is the case will be one of the topics for discussion in this chapter. In addition, we will review important writing dos and don'ts, the importance of establishing a format, as well as appropriate language selection.

If you are like Rob, perhaps by the end of this chapter, you will view the process of writing performance appraisals as less of a chore and more as a useful tool in maximizing employer-employee relations.

WHY WRITTEN PERFORMANCE APPRAISALS ARE IMPORTANT

Effectively written performance appraisals leave little room for misinterpretation by either the employee or the manager. When the written word works in concert with what the appraising manager says during the face-to-face meeting, the nature and level of an employee's performance is reinforced.

Written appraisals become a permanent record attesting to an employee's performance for a specified period of time. This record is often used to:

- Justify salary increases
- Support transfers, promotions, or other changes in job status
- Support disciplinary action, up to and including termination

Let's examine each of these uses more closely.

Justify Salary Increases

It is not uncommon for organizations to link salary increases with annual performance reviews. Furthermore, pay raises are usually driven by merit. Hence, employees receiving high performance ratings are going to anticipate increases in pay commensurate with those ratings.

Let's look at how this might work. Donna is the human resources representative responsible for reviewing her organization's performance appraisals once they have been completed and submitted by managers. Her job includes looking for consistency between comments and ratings for each category, as well as consistency between the overall rating/comments and all those ratings/comments preceding it. Once a manager has met with his or employee, and the employee has signed the review (indicating understanding of its contents and not necessarily agreement), Donna places her salary increase chart along side the completed review. Each of her company's four-term rating's reflects a corresponding percentage salary increase: Extraordinary = 5–5.5%, Excellent = 4–4.5%, Good = a maximum of 3%, and Poor = 0%. (Note: if an employee receives a "poor" rating in multiple categories and an overall rating of "poor," one has to ask why he or she is still on payroll.)

If Donna finds consistency throughout each of the appraisal categories, culminating in an overall evaluation that supports the preceding ratings, her job is easy. If, however, there is a lack of uniformity between categories and the final rating seems out of kilter, she then needs to confer with the manager. Generally, either the individual evaluations or the final rating is inaccurate. Sometimes, however, there is one category that the manager feels should weigh more heavily than all the others; hence, the rating for that competency skews the other scores. This is acceptable if the category is job-specific, HR agrees, and most importantly, if the employee is aware of the additional emphasis on this task of area of responsibility.

Salary-related problems arise when there is a lack of consistency between ratings and pay raises. One of the simplest ways to avoid this inconsistency is for managers to submit written reviews to HR for confirmation of consistency prior to meeting with employees. The ideal solution is to separate salary reviews from performance appraisals. Employees are more likely to focus on the manager's observations and not translate ratings into dollars.

Support Changes in Job Status

Job posting is commonplace in many workplaces, offering employees opportunities for both advancement and lateral transfers to other departments. Performance appraisals act as critical documents in this process, often serving as the main basis for supporting or denying changes in employee job status.

Let's consider some examples:

- Ralph applies for a promotion to a job requiring critical thinking and quick decisions. His most recent performance appraisal provides several examples of instances in which he has made decisions resulting in increased revenues for the company.
- Joseph likes his work, but finds it difficult to get along with his boss. He applies for a transfer to another department where he will perform essentially the same function. The manager of the department with the opening looks at his last performance appraisal and reads the following comment in the category, independence: "Joseph is too independent; he likes to work without a great deal of supervision."

The manager realizes that this was intended to be a criticism, but instead views it in a positive manner: she wants someone who can work independently.

Perhaps the appraiser's comment is part of the problem with the working relationship between himself and Joseph, causing the latter to apply for a transfer.

- Ali's boss is promoted, leaving his job vacant. The person making the replacement selection is the vice president to whom Ali's boss reported: someone with whom she has had little direct contact. Ali applies, believing she can do the work. Unfortunately, her last review tells a different story: she is described as "having difficulty adhering to company policy" and as being "excessively argumentative." There are no examples to support either statement. The vice president can now choose to accept what the performance appraisal says without seeking clarification (not recommended), or contact the former incumbent, asking for specific examples. He should also meet with Ali and form his own opinion, mostly by asking competency-based, open-ended, hypothetical, probing, and close-ended questions. (These types of questions will be discussed in Chapter 6.)

Support Disciplinary Action

One of the most important rules of performance appraisals is that nothing said in writing or during an appraisal meeting should come as a surprise to employees. If managers have addressed disciplinary matters throughout the year via coaching and counseling sessions, then a recap of these instances during the formal review is appropriate. If, however, the manager did not do his or her job as a coach and counselor at the time of an occurrence calling for progressive discipline, then it is inappropriate to record it on the appraisal form or discuss it during the face-to-face meeting for the first time.

Let's continue with the logical progression of what might happen if matters calling for discipline *are* addressed in a timely fashion and subsequently recorded on the performance appraisal form. Should the employee correct the documented behavior, this should be acknowledged. If, however, the behavior continues or escalates, the written performance appraisal becomes an important point of reference. Consider this excerpt from a written review:

> *Category:* Reliability: The extent to which an employee can be relied upon to complete a given task and follow-up as needed
> *Rating:* Poor
> *Comment:* Despite repeated discussions concerning her failure to meet deadlines in a timely manner (see attached memos reflecting coaching and counseling sessions), Danielle continues to consistently turn her work in late. She has been given two verbal warnings (see attached documentation) and understands, as indicated by her signature, that the continuation of this behavior will lead to further disciplinary action up to and including termination.

If Danielle's issue with reliability were not addressed in the written review, despite documentation in her file, any future steps toward disciplinary action could be adversely impacted. This would be especially true if the appraising manager rated her using terms that contradicted coaching and counseling documentation on file.

? Think About It...

Does your organization link salary increases with performance appraisals? _____ yes _____ no

If it does, what happens if there is inconsistency between comments and ratings for each category, and/or inconsistency between the overall rating/comments and all those ratings/comments preceding it? Specifically, what is the impact on an employee's salary?

_____

_____

Does your organization offer employees job change opportunities via job posting?
_____ yes _____ no

If it does, what is the relationship between an employee being considered for a job change and his or her prior performance appraisal?

_____

_____

Does your organization have a progressive disciplinary system? _____ yes _____ no

If it does, what is the relationship between an employee who has been disciplined and his or her upcoming performance appraisal?

_____

_____

If managers were made aware that performance appraisals could be used to justify salary increases, support changes in job status, and back up disciplinary action, do you think they would be less resistant to writing them? _____ yes _____ no. Support your answer.

_____

_____

_____

_____

WHY MANAGERS DISLIKE WRITING PERFORMANCE APPRAISALS

Despite the fact that written performance appraisals can be used to justify salary increases, support changes in job status, and back up disciplinary action, managers still resist. They are quick to offer many reasons for this, including the following:

1. "There's too much to say; I can't possibly fit everything in the space provided."
2. "I have nothing to say; besides, the employee's performance speaks for itself."

3. "I don't write well; after all, I'm a manager—not a writer."
4. "I have a problem with praising people; besides I don't want to embarrass an employee by complimenting him or her too much."
5. "I have a problem with criticizing people; I know I hate being criticized."
6. "It's a thankless task; HR always gets on my case about not doing it right. I've given up trying to please them."
7. "I'm afraid my words will come back to haunt me. What if I'm wrong? Saying something face-to-face is all right—but committing yourself to paper can be dangerous."
8. "It takes too long; who has that kind of time?"
9. "It's hard work, especially when you have to criticize someone."
10. "All employees really care about is how much of a raise they're getting, so why bother?"

In addition to these reasons, managers have reportedly expressed concern about what could happen if they write what they really think. Fill in the blank of the following statement with any of the terms provided to see what many managers have said they are worried about:

If I write what I really think, employees will _____.

- Argue with me
- Bad-mouth me
- Be angry with me
- Become defensive
- Behave disruptively
- Cry
- Lie
- Report me

Think About It...

Of the ten reasons cited for disliking writing performance appraisals, I can relate to (write as many as apply):

_____

_____

I have reasons of my own for disliking writing performance appraisals, including:

_____

_____

I cannot relate to any of this; I like writing performance appraisals because:

_____

_____

_____

- Sulk
- Turn others against me
- Walk out
- Yell

VIEWING WRITTEN PERFORMANCE APPRAISALS AS A USEFUL TOOL

Managers can learn to view writing performance appraisals as less of a chore and more as a useful tool in maximizing effective employer-employee relations by honestly answering three questions. Let's examine those three questions via my experience.

I was conducting a performance appraisal seminar for a group of managers whom I knew would resist the idea of writing reviews. After talking briefly about the benefits of written appraisals, it was evident that I was not making any headway. This audience was simply not buying any of my persuasive talk, so I decided on a different approach. Instead of telling them why written performance appraisals were so beneficial, I asked three questions:

Question #1: "Who likes writing performance appraisals?" I queried. Not surprisingly, no one raised his or her hand.

Question #2: "Who thinks written performance appraisals are important?" Again, I was not surprised to see that this time everyone's hand went up. I smiled and summarized, "You don't like writing them but agree that they're important; that's interesting."

Question #3: "Who thinks someone else should write the appraisals then?" The room was initially quiet; then some of the managers started murmuring to one another. I asked someone to volunteer what he or she was thinking. "I don't like the idea of someone else writing a review for one of my employees—I'm the only one who really knows what they can and can't do," said one manager. Others nodded in agreement. Another said, "I'd like to tell someone what I think and have him or her write it." "What kind of sense does that make?" challenged a colleague. "If you're going to take the time to talk about it, just write it down!"

This exchange continued for about ten minutes, at which point I asked volunteers to summarize what they had concluded. Without hesitation, here's what they collectively said: (Note: the word "it" refers to the written performance appraisal.) (1) Managers should just do it! (2) Managers should learn how to do it right! (3) If managers learn how to do it, and do it right, it's a win-win situation for everyone! I could not have agreed more.

THE IMPORTANCE OF ESTABLISHING A FORMAT

The success of any performance appraisal system is rooted in consistency and uniformity; that is, all managers following the same format. This concept extends to the written review. Employees need to know that they are being evaluated according to the same standards as everyone else, that their salary increases are based on the same factors, and that ratings used to gauge the extent of their accomplishments are the same ones used to evaluate the accomplishments of their coworkers.

A Seven-Step Format

The following seven-step format for written performance appraisals (Exhibit 5–1) is simple, yet highly effective when it comes to ensuring consistency and uniformity. The approach is applicable to virtually every workplace, is appropriate for all employee classifications, and works with any type of appraisal form, regardless of the categories included. Optimum results will be achieved if self-evaluations by employees are factored in as well.

Step 1: Overview. Provide a two-to-three sentence summary of the employee's performance since his or her last review or date of hire. Avoid referencing specific incidences. Here's an example:

> *Since the date of her last annual review, Veronica has continued to exhibit an in-depth understanding of her job. She consistently performs her responsibilities in an exemplary fashion, serving as a role model for new hires.*

Step 2: Strengths. Identify employee strengths, supported by specific examples. Try to highlight examples reflecting a variety of assignments performed under varying circumstances throughout the year. Try also to reflect different strengths, especially those reflecting growth and development since the time of hire or the last review.

Step 3: Areas Requiring Improvement. Identify areas in which the employee requires improvement, supported by specific examples. Be careful not to preface any statements with terminology like, "I think . . . " or "In my opinion. . .."

 **Think About It...**

Can you think of any reason as to why a consistent and uniform written performance appraisal format would not work in your organization?

_____

_____

_____

What could be done to eliminate this reason from interfering with a uniform and consistent written performance appraisal format in your organization?

_____

_____

_____

_____

E **xhibit 5–1**
Seven-Step Format for Written Performance Appraisals

Step 1: Overview
Provide a summary of the employee's performance since his or her last review or date of hire.

Step 2: Strengths
Identify employee strengths, supported by specific examples.

Step 3: Areas Requiring Improvement
Identify areas in which the employee requires improvement, supported by specific examples.

Step 4: Meeting Previously Agreed-Upon Goals
Review the employee's success in meeting specific goals that were mutually agreed-upon at the time of the last review or time of hire.

Step 5: Setting New Goals
Identify new, mutually agreed-upon goals for the employee to achieve accompanied by a timeline.

Step 6: Career Development
Together, identify how the employee will achieve personal and professional development.

Step 7: Employee Feedback
Solicit the employee's written comments on the performance appraisal form accompanied by his or her signature.

Areas requiring improvement should be job-specific, as well as tangible or quantitative.

Citing examples of areas requiring improvement can lend itself to a discussion of setting goals *(Step 5)*.

Step 4: Meeting Previously Agreed-Upon Goals. Review the employee's success in meeting specific goals that were mutually agreed-upon at the time of the last review or time of hire. Cite the goal; then specify exactly what the employee did or did not do toward meeting that goal. Avoid general terms, such as "Richard did a great job meeting all his goals from last year!" or "Jen needs to keep working hard so she can meet the goals she set last year."

Step 5: Setting New Goals. Identify mutually agreed-upon goals for the employee to accomplish by the date of his or her next appraisal. Goals should be clear, measurable, time-tied, and focused on results. For example, "Launch four new testing programs in the coming fiscal year" is clear, measurable, time-tied, and focuses on results.

Develop a timeline with interim meetings set to review progress and identify any problems encountered by the employee as he or she strives to meet these goals. New goals may also include a carry-over of goals from the last meeting. Revisit and rework them as needed, ensuring that they are achievable and desirable from the employee's perspective.

While goals should be mutually agreed-upon, managers play a greater role in specifying goals for work that is primarily prefigured; that is, routine,

Think About It...

Do the managers in your organization consistently and uniformly practice the seven-step format for written performance appraisals?

Step 1: Overview	_____ yes _____ no
Step 2: Strengths	_____ yes _____ no
Step 3: Areas Requiring Improvement	_____ yes _____ no
Step 4: Meeting Previously Agreed-Upon Goals	_____ yes _____ no
Step 5: Setting New Goals	_____ yes _____ no
Step 6: Career Development	_____ yes _____ no
Step 7: Employee Feedback	_____ yes _____ no

If you answered "no" for any of the steps, what do you think it would take to help managers consistently and uniformly practice the seven-step format for written performance appraisals?

_____

_____

_____

repetitive tasks. Managers generally solicit goals from the employee for work that is primarily configured; that is, non-routine tasks. Hence:

Task		Manager's Role
Prefigured	routine, repetitive	Emphasis on specifying goals
Configured	non-routine	Emphasis on soliciting goals

Step 6: Career Development. Managers should encourage employees to discuss career goals and aspirations. Together, they can then identify how the employee will achieve personal and professional development, for example, through seminars, training, and schooling. These goals should be linked, as much as possible, with organizational goals.

Step 7: Employee Feedback. Solicit employee signatures and written comments on the performance appraisal form. As stated earlier, their signature signifies understanding of the contents and not necessarily agreement. Their comments, while unlikely to result in a changed evaluation, can serve to enhance future employer-employee relations.

WRITING GUIDELINES

Conveying the right tone and using an appropriate writing style will set the stage for a productive face-to-face meeting. Simply stated, your tone should be direct, factual, and positive; your style should be moderate to formal, with limited jargon and no clichés.

Writing Dos

Here are some additional guidelines to help managers write effective performance reviews:

1. *Do* begin planning the written performance appraisal approximately one month prior to the due date, jotting down thoughts as they occur to you.
2. *Do* write the review and then put it away for a few days. Return to it and read it from multiple perspectives, including your own, that of the employee, and that of human resources.
3. *Do* use the employee's position description as the foundation for your written review, striving to link each comment with specific job duties and responsibilities.
4. *Do* support each rating with multiple examples and facts.
5. *Do* be prepared to discuss supporting examples.
6. *Do* try to present a balanced picture of strengths and areas requiring improvement.
7. *Do* look at an employee's entire performance record since his or her last review, date of hire, or date of most recent job change—whichever applies.
8. *Do* consider the employee's self-evaluation, as well as evaluations solicited from others, such as colleagues and clients.

 **Think About It...**

When managers in your organization write performance appraisals, do they know to

. . . begin planning the written performance appraisal approximately one month prior to the due date? _____ yes _____ no

. . . write the review and then put it away for a few days; then reread it from multiple perspectives? _____ yes _____ no

. . . use the employee's job description as the foundation for their written review? _____ yes _____ no

. . . support each rating with multiple examples and facts? _____ yes _____ no

. . . present a balanced picture of strengths and areas requiring improvement? _____ yes _____ no

. . . look at an employee's entire performance record? _____ yes _____ no

. . . consider the employee's self-evaluation? _____ yes _____ no

. . . consider the evaluations of others? _____ yes _____ no

. . . use language that clearly conveys what is expected and acceptable? _____ yes _____ no

. . . strive for consistency between reviews and salary recommendations? _____ yes _____ no

. . . evaluate performance, not personality? _____ yes _____ no

. . . strive to be honest? _____ yes _____ no

Pat yourself and your organization on the back for all the questions you answered with a "yes"! Then strive to convert the "no's" into "yes's," perhaps via training workshops on effective performance appraisal writing for managers.

9. *Do* ensure that the written review clearly conveys what is expected of the employee, as well as what is acceptable and what is not.

10. *Do* strive for consistency between your evaluation and salary increase recommendations.

11. *Do* evaluate performance, and not personality.

12. *Do* be honest.

Writing Don'ts

1. *Don't* allow superior performance in certain categories to influence your ratings in other categories. For example, an employee's job knowledge may be outstanding, but it does not make up for the fact that he or she is unreliable.

2. *Don't* make up strengths or areas requiring improvement that do not exist for the sake of creating a balanced picture.

3. *Don't* be influenced by first impressions or past performance to the extent that you overlook legitimate performance-related issues.

4. *Don't* use the same words to evaluate all employees.

5. *Don't* use absolutes, such as "always" and "never."

6. *Don't* downplay poor performance because you are concerned about hurting an employee's feelings or worried that an employee will no longer like you after reading his or her review.

7. *Don't* introduce anything new: remember, nothing that is said or written during the performance appraisal process should come as a surprise to an employee.

8. *Don't* play it safe by selecting the middle evaluation term for all performance factors.

 **Think About It...**

Of the all the writing "don'ts" identified, which are the three you believe are practiced most frequently by managers in your organization? Why do you think this is so?

___✗___ Allowing superior performance in certain categories to influence ratings in other categories.

_____ Making up strengths or areas requiring improvement that do not exist.

_____ Being excessively influenced by first impressions or past performance.

_____ Using the same words to evaluate all employees.

_____ Using absolute terminology.

_____ Downplaying poor performance out of concern for the employee's feelings or worry that the manager will fall out of favor with the employee.

___✗___ Introducing something new.

_____ Playing it safe by selecting the middle evaluation term.

_____ Being affected by the "recency factor."

_____ Being swayed by the "similarity factor."

_____ Being influenced by the "sympathy factor."

_____ Saying anything that cannot be supported by facts.

9. *Don't* be affected by the "recency factor"; that is, a tendency to be substantially influenced by recent job performance—whether positive or negative.
10. *Don't* be swayed by the "similarity factor"; that is, a tendency to dole out higher ratings to those whose views or characteristics are similar to your own.
11. *Don't* be influenced by the "sympathy factor"; that is, an inclination to overlook performance issues because of personal issues.
12. *Don't* say anything that cannot be supported by facts.

LANGUAGE SELECTION

Language selected for written performance appraisals should be objective. Objective words are impartial and likely to be interpreted similarly by most people. On the other hand, subjective language reflects one's personal opinion, may be subject to interpretation, and fails to communicate relevant, concrete information. An example of an objective statement concerning "job knowledge" would be, "Jill possesses the practical and technical knowledge required for this job." An example of a subjective statement would be, "I think Jill has what it takes to do this job!"

Subjective language that is supported by specific, job-related facts can be made objective. For example, consider the subjective statement, "I think John is very productive." It can be made objective in the following way: "I think John is very productive in that he frequently has his station ready on time."

Objective language can be used to evaluate outstanding, average, and marginal employees. Here are three examples of objective comments appearing on a performance appraisal form for the category "Job Knowledge:"

Outstanding Employee: Carolyn demonstrates an in-depth understanding of both the practical and technical knowledge needed to perform her job, far exceeding that which is required. She is also willing to impart that knowledge to coworkers having difficulty understanding certain aspects of their jobs. (Note: specific examples would elaborate on instances in which Carolyn has helped coworkers.)

Average Employee: Clarke demonstrates a sound understanding of the practical knowledge required for his job, but resists help with certain technical aspects in which he is not as well versed. This, in turn, occasionally prevents him from completing his work in a timely fashion. (Note: specific examples would elaborate on instances in which Clarke's diminished technical knowledge has prevented him from completing his work on time.)

Marginal Employee: Lana possesses a marginally acceptable level of knowledge with which to perform her job, with her technical knowledge slightly outweighing her practical knowledge. This is not due to a lack of effort on her part; she simply does not seem to grasp the fundamentals required to perform her work. This has resulted in other employees having to perform some of her tasks, producing a growing morale problem.

(Note: specific examples would elaborate on examples of Lana's effort to become more knowledgeable about her job, as well as to describe specific instances in which Lana's limited job knowledge has resulted in other employees having to do her work in addition to their own.)

✎ Exercise: Objective and Subjective Language

Look at the following words in relation to the eleven performance appraisal factors in the left-hand column. If you believe the statement is objective, put a check mark in the "Objective or Subjective" column. If you feel the statement is subjective, reword it so that it is objective. (Note: indicating that a statement is objective does not mean it can or should stand alone; the addition of supporting facts or examples is presumed.)

Factor	Comment	Objective or Subjective
Quality	No one could do this job better!	
Productivity	Makes too many mistakes	
Job Knowledge	Acceptable understanding of the job	
Reliability	Would never let you down	
Attendance	No absences; always on time	
Independence	Crumbles without direction	
Creativity	Not very creative	
Initiative	Needs to take more initiative	
Adherence to Policy	Doesn't always follow policies	
Interpersonal Relationships	Has lots of friends at all levels	
Judgment	Can be counted on to exercise good judgment	

HINTS, SUGGESTIONS, AND SOME ANSWERS

Factor	Comment	Objective or Subjective
Quality	No one could do this job better!	Extremely conscientious and diligent worker
Productivity	Makes too many mistakes	Number of errors is considerably higher than average
Job Knowledge	Acceptable understanding of the job	√
Reliability	Would never let you down	Very reliable
Attendance	No absences; always on time	√
Independence	Crumbles without direction	Requires close supervision and detailed directions
Creativity	Not very creative	Fails to come up with alternative ways of approaching tasks

Initiative	Needs to take more initiative	√
Adherence to Policy	Doesn't always follow policies	√
Interpersonal Relationships	Interacts well with people at all levels	√
Judgment	Can be counted on to exercise good judgment	√

Written performance appraisals are important for several reasons. When effectively prepared, they leave little room for misinterpretation by either the employee or the manager. In addition, when the written word works in concert with what the appraising manager says during the face-to-face meeting, the nature and level of an employee's performance is reinforced.

Written appraisals also become a permanent record attesting to an employee's performance for a specified period of time. This record is often used to justify salary increases, support transfers, promotions, or other changes in job status, as well as support disciplinary action, up to and including termination.

Many managers resist writing performance appraisals, despite their many uses. They cite numerous reasons for this resistance, including concern that what they write will come back to haunt them, apprehension connected with criticizing others, and worry over not being able to write well. Managers can learn to view writing performance appraisals as less of a chore and more as a useful tool in maximizing effective employer-employee relations by acknowledging the fact that they best know what employees can and cannot do.

The success of any performance appraisal system is rooted in consistency and uniformity; that is, all managers following the same format. This concept extends to the written review. Employees need to know that they are being evaluated according to the same standards as everyone else, that their salary increases are based on the same factors, and that ratings used to gauge the extent of their accomplishments are the same used to evaluate the accomplishment of their coworkers. A simple, yet highly effective seven-step format helps managers achieve optimum results.

Conveying a certain tone and using a particular style will set the stage for a maximally productive face-to-face meeting. Simply stated, your tone should be direct and positive, and your style moderate to formal.

Language selected for written performance appraisals should be factual, job-related, specific, and objective. Objective words are impartial and likely to be interpreted similarly by most people. On the other hand, subjective language reflects one's personal opinion, may be subject to interpretation, and fails to communicate relevant, concrete information. Subjective language that is supported by specific, job-related facts can be made objective.

Review Questions

1. The purpose of the important, tone-setting, first step in the
   seven-step appraisal-writing format is to:
   (a) identify employee strengths and areas requiring
       improvement, supported by specific examples.
   (b) provide a summary of the employee's performance
       since his or her last review or date of hire.
   (c) determine how successful the employee has been in
       meeting mutually agreed-upon goals at the time of the
       last review or time of hire.
   (d) ascertain agreement from the employee that he or
       she will ultimately provide support for the contents of
       the written review via his or her signature.

   1. (b)

2. Managers can turn performance appraisal writing into a
   win-win situation for all concerned if they:
   (a) let human resources write the reviews.
   (b) rely on employee self-appraisals.
   (c) accept the fact that written reviews are useful tools.
   (d) refrain from saying anything negative.

   2. (c)

3. Objective language is used to evaluate:
   (a) outstanding, average, and marginal employees.
   (b) average employees only.
   (c) marginal employees only.
   (d) outstanding employees only.

   3. (a)

4. Written performance appraisals become a permanent record
   attesting to an employee's performance for a specified period
   of time. This record is often used to justify salary increases,
   support disciplinary action, and:
   (a) support changes in job status.
   (b) make the manager look good.
   (c) justify the need for additional human resources.
   (d) support what is said during the face-to-face meeting.

   4. (a)

Do you have questions? Comments? Need clarification?
Call Educational Services at 1-800-225-3215, ext. 600,
or email at ed_svcs@amanet.org.

5. The "similarity factor" refers to:

    (a) the relationship between an employee's review and the manager's recommendation for a salary increase.

    (b) the correlation between what a manager writes and what he or she says during the appraisal meeting.

    (c) the like rating of several employees working in a similar capacity.

    (d) a tendency to dole out higher ratings to those whose views or characteristics are similar to one's own.

5. (d)

6

Conducting the Performance Appraisal Meeting

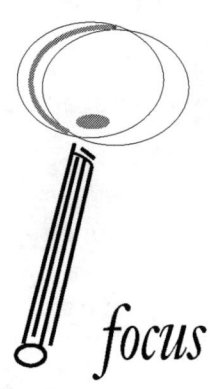

focus

Learning Objectives

By the end of this chapter, you should be able to:

- Apply effective interviewing skills to the face-to-face performance appraisal meeting between managers and employees.
- Identify key areas to be covered in a performance appraisal meeting.
- Overcome typical performance appraisal meeting pitfalls.
- Conduct negative appraisal meetings.
- Effectively conclude the appraisal meeting.

I once polled a group of more than one hundred middle managers from several work environments on their views concerning the face-to-face performance appraisal meeting. One of the questions I posed was: "On a scale of 1 to 10, with 10 representing "very comfortable," 5 signifying "reasonably comfortable," and 1 meaning "extremely uncomfortable," how would your rate your level of comfort in conducting face-to-face performance appraisal meetings with your employees?"

Only four respondents said they were very comfortable conducting appraisal meetings; seven managers answered with a "1." Since the majority fell into the "reasonably comfortable" range, I followed up with the logical question of why they answered the way they did. More specifically, I asked these managers what made them uncomfortable about conducting face-to-face performance appraisal meetings. Their reasons included: "It's hard to tell someone the truth about their performance when it's negative;" "I don't want to be the bad guy;" "I never know what to say;" "What's the point? All that really matters to them is how much of a raise they're getting" and "Employees know how they're doing—I don't need to point out the obvious."

It is hard to argue with the logic of these statements, but it does not have to be this way. Managers can learn to view performance appraisal meetings as a means to an end: that is, as a way for employees to improve their skills and for both parties to enhance employer-employee relations. The way to do this is for managers to increase their comfort level with the interview process by learning and applying effective interviewing skills, becoming familiar and comfortable with areas to be covered, identifying and avoiding common pitfalls, and knowing how to end the meeting. For some managers, the most important step toward increasing one's comfort level with the interview is to become more skilled at conducting negative appraisal meetings.

EFFECTIVE INTERVIEWING SKILLS

Becoming comfortable with conducting face-to-face performance appraisal meetings begins with successfully applying effective interviewing skills.

Setting the Stage

Setting the stage for the face-to-face appraisal meeting between managers and employees is beneficial to both groups in that it ensures coverage of all the necessary meeting components and assures employees of a comprehensive exchange of information.

While both parties obviously know why they are meeting, the manager's opening remarks set the tone for what follows, as well as alerting the employee as to what he or she can expect over the next hour or so. Here are two examples of how a manager might begin:

- "Hi, Frank; have a seat. I'm glad you're here; I'm looking forward to talking with you about your performance over the past year. We'll also look at

Think About It...

On a scale of 1–10, with 10 representing "very comfortable," 5 signifying "reasonably comfortable," and 1 meaning "extremely uncomfortable," how would your rate your level of comfort in conducting face-to-face performance appraisal meetings with your employees?

Why?

some of your goals for the upcoming year. This is *your* review, Frank, so please feel free to comment or ask questions at any point. Ready?"

- Good morning, Frank. Please, have a seat. I trust you've completed your self-appraisal, as requested. I have my review of your work over the past year, which I'll be comparing with your self-review. In keeping with our 360-degree appraisal approach, I also have input from some of your colleagues and clients with whom you regularly work, which we'll review. After that, we'll discuss how successful you've been in meeting the goals we agreed to the last time we met, as well as new performance goals and your career aspirations. I invite you to comment or ask questions along the way. Let's begin, all right?"

As you can see, the manager's opening remarks in these two examples suggest two entirely different approaches. The manager in the first example has a casual style, setting the stage for an informal meeting. Our second manager is more reserved, suggesting a more structured, formalized meeting. Both approaches have accomplish the desired goal: that is, to let employees know what to expect.

Different Types of Interview Questions

Practicing effective interviewing skills includes the ability to differentiate between types of interview questions and knowing when to use one over the other. (See Exhibit 6–1.)

Competency-Based Questions

Competency-based questions focus on specific examples drawn from four key categories: tangible or measurable abilities, knowledge, behavior, and interpersonal skills. Most jobs emphasize one category over the other, but every employee should be able to demonstrate competencies in all four categories to some extent.

When asking competency-based questions during a performance appraisal meeting, managers should focus on relating specific past job performance to probable future on-the-job behavior. For example: "Kay, as we've discussed on several occasions, you've had a great deal of difficulty

---

? **Think About It...**

Indicate the style you prefer when making opening remarks: _____ casual _____ formal

Do you think your style could have an impact on the outcome of the performance appraisal meeting? _____ yes _____ no. Explain your answer.

_____

_____

_____

xhibit 6–1
Different Types of Interview Questions

Competency-Based Questions:
Focus on relating specific past job performance to probable future on-the-job behavior.

Open-Ended Questions:
Require full, multiple-word responses, lending themselves to discussion.

Hypothetical Questions:
Based on anticipated or known job-related tasks.
Questions are phrased in the form of problems and presented to the employee for solutions.

Probing Questions:
Allow managers to delve more deeply for additional information.
Best thought of as follow-up questions, they are usually short and simply worded.

Close-Ended Questions:
May be answered with a single word—generally "yes" or "no."
Can give the manager greater control, put certain employees at ease, are useful when seeking clarification, are helpful when you need to verify information, and usually result in concise responses.

---

meeting deadlines; put in more general terms, you've had trouble with time management. Let's talk about a specific instance when you had plenty of advance notice as to when a project was due, but still couldn't complete it on time. What do you think went wrong?" (Allow the employee ample time to respond fully.) Now continue by saying, "Let's look ahead: imagine receiving that exact same assignment next week. What would you do differently? That is, what technical abilities, knowledge, behavior, and interpersonal skills can you draw upon to ensure timely completion?" As the employee talks, the manager should jot down notes, effectively developing a time management plan for the employee to implement. This can become part of the employee's future performance goals.

Open-Ended Questions
By definition, open-ended questions require full, multiple-word responses. Open-ended questions generally lend themselves to discussion and result in information upon which the manager can build additional questions. They encourage employees to talk, thereby allowing the manager to actively listen and assess both verbal and nonverbal responses. Open-ended questions are particularly helpful in encouraging shy or quiet employees to talk without the pressure that can accompany competency-based questions requiring specific examples.

In performance appraisal meetings, open-ended questions are especially productive during that portion dedicated to discussing future goals and career development. Here are two samples:

- "You've certainly succeeded in meeting all of the goals set at our last appraisal meeting. Building on those successes and looking ahead, what performance objectives do you see yourself achieving over the next year?"
- "Let's talk a bit about your future goals. I know you've been taking computer classes at our local community college; how do you see computers fitting in with your career plans?"

Hypothetical Questions

Hypothetical questions are based on anticipated or known job-related tasks. The questions are phrased in the form of problems and presented to the employee for solutions. These questions allow for the evaluation of reasoning abilities, thought processes, attitudes, creativity, work style, and one's approach to different tasks.

Let's consider this example from an appraisal meeting during which the employee, currently a first-line supervisor, expresses an interest in furthering her career by becoming a manager. You have a complete understanding of how well she performs in her current capacity, but need more information about how she is likely to deal with managerial responsibilities.

Here is a relevant hypothetical question: "If you were a manager, and your team complained about having to meet some rather unreasonable demands from one of the company's top clients, how would you go about satisfying both the client and your staff?"

Probing Questions

These are questions that allow managers to delve more deeply for additional information. Best thought of as follow-up questions, they are usually short and simply worded. Probing questions are appropriate when discussing past performance, previously set objectives, new performance objectives, and career development plans. Here are some examples:

- "You mentioned that the last project you participated in didn't turn out the way you'd planned. *What happened?*"
- "You've succeeded in meeting the goals you set last year; *what do you attribute this to?*"
- "You indicated that you'd like to try your hand at marketing; *why?*"
- "Who or what has influenced you with regard to your career goals? *In what way?*"

Close-Ended Questions

These are questions that may be answered with a single word—generally "yes" or "no." Close-ended questions can give the manager greater control, put certain employees at ease, are useful when seeking clarification, are helpful when you need to verify information, and usually result in concise responses. On the other hand, close-ended questions can result in limited information and should not be used in lieu of competency-based, open-ended, hypothetical, or probing questions.

Here are some examples of functional close-ended questions. In each instance, the response will serve as the foundation for one of the other types of interview questions.

- "Would you say that your rapport with your coworkers has been impacted as a result of your role as team leader on the last project?"
- "Earlier you said that your inability to come in on time is due to the fact that the bus schedule has been changed; have you ever considered taking an earlier bus or using another mode of transportation?"

✎ Exercise: Interview Questions

Consider this scenario: You are meeting with Joe for his annual performance appraisal. Joe has effectively worked as your assistant for the past two years. You have given him an overall rating of "very good"—the second highest possible rating. Joe has expressed an interest in taking on additional responsibilities.

As his manager, identify five questions you would ask Joe during the appraisal meeting:

Competency-based question:

_____

_____

Open-ended question:

_____

_____

Hypothetical question:

_____

_____

Probing question:

_____

_____

Close-ended question:

_____

_____

HINTS, SUGGESTIONS, AND SOME ANSWERS

Competency-based question:
"Joe, taking on additional responsibilities requires good time management skills. Tell me about a specific instance in which you had to juggle multiple assignments, all due at the same time. How did you allocate your time?"

Open-ended question:
"Please describe three of your greatest strengths and how you feel they qualify you for taking on additional responsibilities."

Hypothetical question:
"Consider this scenario: You're a supervisor in charge of four employees, two of whom do not get along. Their bickering is impacting productivity and the morale of their coworkers. What would you do?"

Probing question:
"You indicated earlier that you want to return to college; *what courses are you interested in taking?*"

Close-ended question:
"Based on what you have told me so far, can I assume that your ultimate goal is to become the manager of this department?"

Talking Versus Listening

Managers need to balance the amount of talking they do with listening. Many managers talk too much, erroneously believing that they are more in control of the meeting as long as they are talking. In reality, managers should devote no more than twenty-five percent of the time to talking. Their time should be spent highlighting and asking questions about the employee's past performance and success in achieving previously set performance objectives. In addition, they should ask questions about the employee's new performance objectives and career development plans. The remaining seventy-five percent of the meeting should be devoted to listening to the employee.

Guidelines for effective listening include:

- Listening for connecting themes to enable you to concentrate on key job-related information
- Summarizing periodically to ensure a clear picture of what the employee is telling you
- Filtering out distractions to avoid missing important information
- Using information as the basis for additional questions
- Screening out personal biases
- Acknowledging any unusual emotional states that could influence your ability to concentrate

✎ Exercise: Talking Versus Listening

Imagine conducting a performance appraisal meeting with an employee who, while competent, is not very interesting to listen to. He speaks in a monotone, and tends to ramble. What listening guidelines could you apply that would enable you to focus and more actively listen?

_____

_____

_____

Body Language

Managers and employees can learn as much about one another through their body language as from verbal messages. On the other hand, nonverbal messages are easily misinterpreted, generally when body language is interpreted according to the other person's own gestures or expressions. For example, just because you have a tendency to avoid eye contact when you are hiding something does not mean that an employee is avoiding your eyes for the same reason.

Each of us has our own pattern of communicating nonverbally. This includes facial expressions, body movements and gestures, as well as pauses in speech, rate of speech, vocal tone, pitch, and enunciation. Together, all of these factors "speak" to another person from the very first moment of contact. Often the message can be confusing. For example, body movements such as finger or foot tapping can contradict facial expressions such as smiling. The situation may be further complicated when the manager tries to assess the content of what is being said. The conflict between the verbal and nonverbal message can be confusing, leaving the manager wondering which message is more accurate. Here is a tip: Since verbal messages are clearly easier to control than nonverbal ones, when there is a conflict between the verbal and the nonverbal, the nonverbal is often more persuasive. This may be helpful, however, only to the extent that the person's nonverbal messages are being interpreted accurately.

During a performance appraisal meeting, a manager should strive to accomplish three goals:

1. *To convey positive body language* by exhibiting gestures and movements that are typically interpreted as positive, such as leaning forward in one's seat when the other person is speaking.

2. *To project consistency between verbal and nonverbal messages* by focusing on using clear language supported by typically interpreted gestures. For example, if a manager wants to express encouragement, she could say, "I think your goal of becoming a supervisor is achievable; let's talk about what you need to do to get there." At the same time, she could maintain direct eye contact, smile, and sit up straight in her chair, appearing ready to discuss the employee's interest in upward mobility.

3. *To accurately assess nonverbal messages conveyed by the employee* by looking for individual patterns. For example, the employee who rubs his eyes every time you broach the subject of how he is doing with a current long-term project, is conveying a pattern that suggests something is amiss. It is likely that this individual rubs his eyes whenever he is uncomfortable or feels he is being pressed to discuss something he would prefer to avoid. This pattern alerts you to the fact that you need to probe deeper and persist until you determine what is really going on.

Let's look at a scenario that encapsulates these three objectives: Liz is meeting with her manager, Anne, to discuss her annual performance appraisal. A preliminary examination of her review reveals what she expected: consistently high ratings in every category. As Anne delves into the details of each area her body language is supportive and encouraging, including direct eye contact and leaning forward. When Liz speaks Anne nods, indicating understanding. When it comes time to discuss Liz's future aspirations, Anne listens carefully then says, "I hear what you're saying Liz, about wanting to continue growing in your current position, but I can't help but wonder if there isn't something more you'd like to strive to accomplish."

Anne is responding to the inconsistency between Liz's body language and her words. She is specifically responding to the fact that she began shifting in her seat and hunched over when the subject turned to her career objectives. Anne does not assign a specific meaning to either movement; however, the sudden change in Liz's body language sends a message to Anne that something is amiss. Sure enough, Liz straightens up in her seat and cautiously begins to describe her ultimate career goal. Anne is careful to convey positive body language coupled with encouraging verbal language as Liz gains greater confidence and reveals more details about her dream job.

AREAS TO BE COVERED

The performance appraisal meeting should focus on four key areas: past performance, previously set performance objectives, new performance objec-

---

Think About It...

How do you convey the following messages nonverbally?

Concern: _____

Disagreement: _____

Disapproval: _____

Disbelief: _____

Encouragement: _____

Frustration: _____

Interest: _____

Sincerity: _____

Support: _____

Do you think your nonverbal messages are clear and accurately interpreted?
_____ yes _____ no

Do you consciously strive for consistency between your nonverbal and verbal messages?
_____ yes _____ no

Do you think you know your employees well enough to be able to assess their nonverbal messages accurately? _____ yes _____ no

---

tives, and the employee's career development plan. Stated another way, two areas of focus have to do with what has already taken place, and the other two areas have to do with what is yet to come. Throughout the process, the manager's role should be that of a facilitator.

Past Performance

Many managers erroneously believe that past performance should receive the greatest degree of attention in the appraisal meeting. Indeed, some managers view this as an opportunity to dwell on what the employee has done wrong. However, talking about past performance should take the least amount of time. If the manager is performing his or her coaching and counseling duties effectively throughout the year (Chapter 2), then nothing said during the appraisal meeting will come as a surprise to the employee. The employee should essentially know from the outset how he or she is going to be evaluated.

The manager can use the appraisal meeting as an opportunity to enhance his or her review with input from the employee via a self-evaluation, and/or supplemental information from others as a result of a 360-degree review (both discussed in earlier chapters). This, in turn, should result in a two-way dialogue, with the employee being encouraged to ask questions and freely express himself or herself, both verbally and nonverbally. This dialogue should conclude with a summary of the employee's past performance and the employee's signature on the evaluation form signifying understanding of the contents and not necessarily agreement.

Previously Set Performance Objectives

Discussing how successful the employee has been in achieving previously set performance objectives is the next step in the appraisal meeting. As with past performance, if the manager has done his or her job throughout the year, the employee will have a clear sense of how successful he or she has been in meeting his or her goals prior to this meeting. Presumably, the two will have sat down together at given intervals to discuss progress and/or problems encountered. Perhaps the original goals were adjusted upward or downward. In any event, employees should arrive at these meetings knowing how successful they have been in achieving past goals; what problems, if any, they

 **Think About It...**

If you were an employee on the receiving end of a performance appraisal, how would you feel if your manager dwelled on past performance and previously set performance objectives?

_____

_____

encountered in their quest to satisfy their goals; and how the manager views their accomplishments. This portion of the meeting is a recap, essentially serving as a foundation for setting new performance objectives.

New Performance Objectives

New performance objectives should be predicated on how successful the employee has been in accomplishing past performance objectives. The goal, however, is not necessarily to achieve more or to work harder. Sometimes, new objectives take the employee in an entirely different direction.

To illustrate, Nicholas is a sales agent who increased revenues in his division by twenty-five percent. Since his target was twenty percent, no one would argue that Nicholas had succeeded in meeting his previously set performance objectives. Now it is time for Nicholas to work jointly with his manager to set new performance objectives. At first glance, it might seem logical to suggest that Nicholas strive to increase sales by thirty to thirty-five percent, but that is not what he wants. For the next review period, Nicholas would like to set his sights on becoming more creative in his sales approach. This is slightly problematic as it is not as quantifiable; yet, it is clear that this performance objective will satisfy Nicholas' drive to grow in his job.

Together, Nicholas and his manager should identify a plan for achieving this objective. Here are the steps they will need to take, accompanied by examples of what Nicholas might consider:

1. Clearly state the performance objective. For example: "To become more creative in my sales approach."
2. Break it down into identifiable and manageable components. For example: "To identify and explore various methods for closing deals, to observe other sales approaches first-hand, to practice various sales approaches in a simulated environment, and to isolate those sales approaches that will generate increased sales."
3. Assign resources needed to accomplish each component. For example: "Read periodicals and have conversations with other sales agents will help me explore new methods for closing deals, accompanying other agents on sales calls will enable me to observe varying sales approaches first-hand, having access to a "practice" environment with colleagues present will allow me to experiment with different sales approaches, and talking with my manager about creative sales approaches that will also generate increased sales will help me pinpoint those new approaches that are likely to lead to the achievement of my goal."
4. Identify possible barriers. For example: "Lack of willingness or availability of other sales agents who can demonstrate different sales approaches, lack of a simulated environment in which I can practice and colleagues willing to provide feedback, and my inability to couple creative approaches with increased sales."
5. Develop a timeline that will include periodic meetings between Nicholas and his manager. For example, assuming the initial meeting between Nicholas and his manager takes place on February 15, on March 12: "Meet

with my manager to report on what I've learned about different methods for closing deals; on April 30, meet to summarize my first-hand observations of other sales approaches; on May 5, practice various sales approaches in a simulated environment with colleagues present to provide feedback; on May 21, meet with my manager to identify those sales approaches that we jointly determine will likely generate increased sales while allowing me to be more creative in my approach."

Remember, the manager's role throughout this process is that of a facilitator. He or she can ask questions and make suggestions, but the employee needs to do most of the planning and work.

 **xhibit 6–2**

Employee Career Development Plan

(To be completed by the employee's manager)

Employee Name: _____

Date of Hire: _____

Employment History:

_____

_____

Current Position: _____

Department: _____

Career Goal: _____

Education Needed: _____

Training Needed: _____

Experience Needed: _____

Relevant Strengths and Abilities:

_____

_____

Developmental Opportunities Available in Current Position:

_____

_____

Correlation between Career Goals and Organizational Goals: _____

Realistic Target Date: _____

Signed: _____   Date: _____

_____

xhibit 6–3

Employee Career Development Plan

(To be completed by the employee)

Name: _____

Current Position: _____

Department: _____

Career Goal: _____

Education Needed: _____

Training Needed: _____

Experience Needed: _____

Relevant Strengths and Abilities:

_____

_____

Sequential Action Steps with Corresponding Projected Timeline:

_____

_____

_____

_____

_____

Realistic Target Date: _____

Signed: _____   Date: _____

Career Development Plans

This is the last stage of the appraisal meeting and in many respects the most rewarding. Savvy managers understand the importance of keeping employees motivated (Chapter 7); developing a career plan as part of the appraisal process is one key way of accomplishing this goal.

For maximum results, this stage requires four steps:

Step One: Toward the end of the appraisal meeting, the manager should initiate a discussion about the employee's career objectives. He or she should listen, encouraging the employee to be as specific as possible. The manager should not try to discourage the employee or suggest that the goals are unrealistic or unachievable.

Step Two: The manager should next produce two forms (Exhibits 6–2 and 6–3): one for the manager to complete and the other for the employee to complete. Each of them will fill out their respective form and bring it with them to a follow-up meeting, usually scheduled for one to two weeks later.

Think About It...

What is likely to happen if an employee's career goals are contrary to organizational goals? For instance, could this lack of compatibility impact productivity?

What is likely to happen if a manager does not think an employee's goals are achievable? For instance, could this result in an adverse impact on employer-employee relations?

What is likely to happen if a manager seriously disagrees with any of the sequential action steps and projected timeline identified by the employee? For instance, could this result in frustration on the part of the employee and possibly result in his resignation?

Step Three: The manager and employee will together review the forms each of them has completed, discussing areas in which they agree and disagree.

Step Four: Together, the manager and employee will identify practical steps for implementation in relation to the employee's current job and role in the organization.

TYPICAL PERFORMANCE APPRAISAL MEETING PITFALLS

Even when they have meticulously prepared a written review including ratings that are backed by specific examples, managers can find themselves influenced by factors during the appraisal meeting to the extent that they may be inclined to change their original evaluations. Once made aware of some of these pitfalls or traps, however, managers are less likely to be influenced to change their original assessment. Managers need to be aware of these tendencies throughout the performance appraisal process, keeping them in mind both before and during face-to-face meetings.

Perhaps the most influential factor of all is past performance. Managers can be easily influenced by good past performance to the extent that they assume it will always continue. Hence, performance "glitches" tend to be rationalized and overlooked. On the other hand, poor past performance can detract from improved performance, causing managers to discount steps toward improvement.

An offshoot of the good/bad past performance issue is the recency factor. As we discussed in Chapter 5, the recency factor operates when a significant positive recent accomplishment stands out, overshadowing an otherwise extensive pattern of poor performance. Likewise, a recent error tends to stand out in the manager's mind, overriding a year's worth of steady performance.

Sometimes, too, managers fall into the trap of comparing employees with one another, thereby granting the "best" of the group the highest possible rating. In reality, that person's performance may warrant no more than an above average rating, and the others somewhat less. In addition to failing to review employees' performance accurately, this manager will have departmental-wide performance issues.

The "blind spot syndrome" can also be problematic when it comes time to conduct an appraisal meeting. Here, the manager excuses those employee's shortcomings that are similar to his or her own. Evaluating the employee honestly would mean confronting one's own deficiencies—something many of us have difficulty doing.

Managers may also have an unofficial "don't like" list that they subconsciously refer to when conducting appraisal meetings. Included on this list are: employees who fail to meet their own personal standards, despite the fact that they meet those set in the job description; employees who challenge or disagree with them; employees who are too independent (or too dependent, whichever the perceived case may be); personality traits decidedly different from their own or the department's "superstar"; and employees whose style differs from their own when they performed that job.

Here are some additional common pitfalls that managers should avoid when conducting performance appraisal meetings:

- Becoming defensive or argumentative.
- Discussing personality traits and attitudes.
- Interrupting the employee as long as he or she is saying something relevant.
- Asking leading questions, such as "Don't you think . . .?"

 **Think About It...**

What trap(s) have you fallen into when conducting performance appraisal meetings?

_____

If you have never conducted an appraisal meeting before, what trap(s) do you see yourself as being most vulnerable to?

_____

_____

What steps will you take in the future to avoid these traps when conducting appraisal meetings?

_____

_____

- Expressing opinions, impressions, and feelings as opposed to sticking with the facts.
- Solving the employee's problems for him or her.
- Making statements such as, "If I were you . . ."
- Engaging in superficial discussions.
- Talking about oneself.
- Talking down to the employee.

CONDUCTING NEGATIVE APPRAISAL MEETINGS

As mentioned in Chapter 4, no one will dispute that it is difficult to tell an employee that their performance is unsatisfactory. Many managers avoid what they perceive to be an inevitable confrontation and opt, instead, to tell the employee that his or her work is satisfactory. They do this, hoping that:

- The employee's performance will improve.
- The employee will transfer or terminate.
- The manager will be promoted and the employee will become someone else's "headache."

In reality, poor performers rarely improve without the coaching and counseling of their managers. Instead, what frequently happens is something like this:

Lucy's job performance is borderline satisfactory. Her manager, Victor, tells her that her work is "good," and gives her a raise. Lucy keeps performing at the same level, either not knowing or caring that her work has really slipped into the category of "unsatisfactory." Victor avoids any coaching or counseling opportunities throughout the year, hoping Lucy will quit but she doesn't. Her annual review rolls around and Victor repeats last year's scenario: he tells her that her work is "good" and gives her another raise. Another year goes by and Victor grows increasingly annoyed with Lucy (and himself for not confronting her), and finally explodes. He calls HR and says that he wants Lucy fired. HR pulls her file and finds a stack of performance appraisals that say her work is good, accompanied by a record of pay increases. HR informs Victor that there is no documentation to support his request to terminate her and that he will have to now begin doing what he should have done three years ago: coach, counsel, and document.

Does this scenario sound familiar to you? Scenarios like this can be avoided in a relatively painless way by following these guidelines:

1. Be honest.
2. Support your statements with facts.
3. Avoid opinions or subjective language.
4. Never personalize any situation.
5. Document everything, both negative and positive.
6. Don't wait a year to tell employees that their work is unsatisfactory.
7. Give employees the benefit of the doubt—initially.

8. Make clear that the expectations you are citing are job-related and not yours personally.
9. Don't expect gratitude.
10. Be honest (it's worth repeating).

✎ Exercise: Conducting a Negative Performance Appraisal Meeting

Following is a partial performance appraisal meeting between Bob, a chief engineer, and Al, his general manager. After reading the excerpt, apply the guidelines listed above and on the previous page to Al's handling of his meeting with Bob and answer the questions that appear at the end.

Al: Bob, I asked you to come in because this is the time of year when I have to evaluate your performance for the past year. I have your performance appraisal in front of me, and I want to tell you what I think of how you're doing. Let me review some of the good points first.

Bob: That's always a good place to start and end, as far as I'm concerned!

Al: One of the items that I have rated you on is customer relations with respect to design and application, and I've checked you off here as outstanding.

Bob: No arguments from me on that one!

Al: The reports from our customers have been full of praise about the kind of help you've given them. I have also rated your technical abilities as outstanding. This is reflected by the high quality of design work that leaves your department, and by the help you've given me on difficult engineering problems.

Bob: I do my best, Al, you know that; I always do my best.

Al: Yes, well, um, yes. O.K. I need to, that is, we need to look at the other side of the coin for a moment. One of the most important reasons for getting together today is that I need to tell you about some of your weaker points.

Bob: Weaker points?

Al: I know you have it in you to overcome these weaknesses, so let's cover some of them.

Bob: Some of them? How many are there?

Al: Oh, that's just an expression. Nothing to worry about.

Bob: Uh huh . . .

Al: First, I'm a little concerned about the lack of supervision you're providing for your three section heads.

Bob: What do you mean?

Al: I've heard some things . . . well, you know, people talk; but I've also looked at the records and noticed a marked increase in turnover within your department. And Joanna, one of your top section heads, has been approached by another firm and is probably going to accept their offer.

Bob: Yes, that's true. Joanna feels sort of stuck here and is not getting the kind of opportunities she'd like; she's bright and ambitious; can't say that I blame her.

Al: Well, Bob, maybe it's more than that. Maybe she's not motivated. It's your responsibility to find things that will interest her.

Bob: I see Joanna everyday. We talk about the work she's doing and how she's doing it. I don't have time to get inside her head and figure out what will make her happy. That's her job. Any other complaints?

Al: Well, actually, I've heard that you don't get involved enough with any of your section heads.

Bob: My door is always open. They know that. And so do you. But I don't have time to hold hands.

Al: Is that why you didn't help Joe when he came and told you he didn't think he could make his last deadline without additional help?

Bob: If Joe isn't sharp enough to figure out how to meet his deadline he shouldn't be in that job. I always managed when I was in that job; he should be able to also. It's not all up to me.

Al: No, of course not. I didn't mean to imply that it was. I'm just pointing it out as one of my areas of concern about your performance. I feel that this problem you have with communication and employer-employee relations is contributing to the increase in turnover and low morale in your department.

Bob: Hold it! Now you're telling me I'm a lousy boss and I'm responsible for people leaving and being down in the dumps because they can't cut it?

Al: That's not what I said. Not exactly, anyway. I'm trying to help you out here, Bob, and you're turning on me.

Bob: Let's just cut to the chase, Al; what's the bottom line here?

Al: Bottom line?

Bob: Yeah, my rating; that's why I'm here, isn't it?

Al: Uh, yes, yes . . . it is. Well, what do you think?

Bob: What do I think?

Al: Yes, about your overall rating . . . what do you think you should get?

Bob: I'm the first to admit there's room for improvement; so I'll hold off on saying I'm outstanding and say my overall rating should be "very good."

Al: Interesting.

Bob: What are you giving me Al?

Al: Ah, well, after listening to what you've said, I can see why you feel a "very good" is appropriate.

Bob: You weren't going to give me less than that, were you Al?

Al: I think we can end this on a positive note, Bob. Let's agree that you're going to work on your people skills and try to reduce turnover.

Bob: How?

Al: We can talk about that another time; you know, give it some thought and come up with a plan that we can go over. You're an asset to this company, Bob.

Bob: An asset with weaknesses?

Al: That's a funny way of putting it; everyone has areas that need work, right?

Bob: Yeah; some more than others, right? There's one thing I've got to ask you Al; why did you wait until now to tell me these things?

Al: This is your annual performance appraisal, Bob; I'm supposed to tell you now; besides, be honest—you knew what I was going to talk about, didn't you? In any event, I'm glad you came in this morning; I hope you've found this session helpful; let's get together again in the next few weeks . . .

Bob: Sure, Al; I can't wait.

Was Al honest with Bob? _____ yes _____ no
Did Al support his statements with facts? _____ yes _____ no
Did Al personalize the situation? _____ yes _____ no
Did Al have documentation? _____ yes _____ no
Did Al make a mistake in waiting until the appraisal to tell Bob that aspects of his work were unsatisfactory? _____ yes _____ no

What, if anything, might Al have done differently?

_____

_____

_____

_____

HINTS, SUGGESTIONS, AND SOME ANSWERS

Was Al honest with Bob? Al was honest with Bob as he accurately conveyed the praise Bob had received from customers. He was also somewhat honest when he began discussing Al's failure to provide adequate supervision to his three section heads. The problem was he was relying largely on hearsay information.

Did Al support his statements with facts? Al became flustered when Bob challenged his statements. As such, Al resorted to making assumptions, offering suggestions, and citing generalizations.

Did Al personalize the situation? Al allowed the meeting to become emotional and personal. For example, when Bob became upset by Al's suggestion that employees were leaving because of his poor communication skills, Al said, "I'm trying to help you out here, Bob, and you're turning on me."

Did Al have documentation? Al's information was based primarily on hearsay.

Did Al make a mistake in waiting until the appraisal to tell Bob that aspects of his work were unsatisfactory? Yes. Nothing that is said during a performance review should come as a surprise to the employee.

What, if anything, might Al have done differently? (1) He should have communicated concerns about Bob's work prior to the review; (2) he should have supported his statements with facts; (3) he should have had specific, concrete documentation reflecting Bob's performance; (3) he should have remained impartial and neutral; (4) he could have allowed Bob to complete a self-appraisal so they could discuss any differences in their respective evaluations; (5) he should have maintained the confidentiality of other employees.

CONCLUDE THE MEETING

Generally speaking, performance appraisal meetings should last anywhere from forty-five to ninety minutes. You will need this amount of time to discuss four main areas: past performance, previously set performance objectives, new performance objectives, and the employee's career development plan. It may be tempting to end a performance appraisal meeting sooner than you should, especially if the employee and the manager see eye-to-eye on everything or if the employee is disagreeable and the manager wants to avoid a confrontation. Apply the following checklist before concluding the appraisal meeting and you will find that there is plenty to cover with every type of employee.

Manager's Checklist

Managers are advised to have a checklist identifying what needs to be covered in the appraisal meeting before concluding (Exhibit 6–4).

1. *Did I summarize past performance?* While the appraisal form probably has an overall rating that summarizes your assessment of the employee's past performance, it is still advisable to verbalize your evaluation. Here are some sample summarizing statements:

   - "Joan, in summary, I'd like to reiterate how pleased I am with your overall work performance. You exhibit a fine work ethic and are especially impressive when motivating your team to meet deadlines."
   - "Rich, we've spent a good deal of time talking about your need to improve with regard to accuracy in your work. You've identified some specific steps that you're going to implement, and we've agreed on a schedule of meetings to discuss your progress. I'm confident that you'll succeed."

2. *Did I review previously set performance objectives?* Determining whether the employee has succeeded in meeting previously set performance objectives will enable you both to move forward in setting new objectives. Ask yourself: Were the previous goals realistic? Achievable? Sufficiently challenging? Interesting for the employee? Consistent with his or her personal goals? Here are some examples of what you can say:

   - "Sasha, the manner in which you tackled last year's goals is truly impressive, and I'm pleased to learn that you found the process to be personally gratifying."
   - "Tiffany, as far as your success in meeting previously set performance objectives is concerned, I'd like to summarize by saying that, despite the fact that you fell somewhat short of your overall goal, you exhibited tremendous effort, and that did not go unnoticed."

 **xhibit 6–4**

Manager's Checklist Prior to Concluding the Appraisal Meeting

❑ Did I summarize past performance?
❑ Did I review previously set performance objectives?
❑ Did we work together to set new performance objectives and agree on follow-up dates to review the employee's progress?
❑ Did I work with the employee on a career development plan?
❑ Did I reinforce praise and end on a positive note?
❑ Did I deliver criticism constructively?
❑ Did I encourage the employee to make comments or ask questions?
❑ Did I reiterate my availability for help and support?

---

3. *Did we work together to set new performance objectives and agree on follow-up dates to review the employee's progress?* How well the employee managed to meet past performance objectives sets the stage for future goals. This is a joint effort, and the manager should be able to make a statement similar to the following before concluding the meeting:

- "Lee, I'm pleased with our discussion about your goals for the upcoming year. We have a timeline of interim steps, and we'll meet to discuss your progress as indicated on that timeline. If you have any questions or concerns prior to our first scheduled meeting, please don't hesitate to come to see me."

4. *Did I work with the employee on a career development plan?* Even the most efficient and dedicated employees are going to feel discouraged if the work they perform does not correlate with their personal career development. Consider this statement before concluding the appraisal meeting:

- "Jack, we've agreed to meet in a week to further discuss your career goal of becoming a leading contributor in the marketing department. I've given you a career development form to complete, and I'll do the same. I'm looking forward to helping you achieve your personal objectives while continuing to making a contribution to this organization."

5. *Did I reinforce praise and end on a positive note?* Obviously this is easier to do with outstanding employees:

- "Jill, I'd like to conclude by reiterating what I've said throughout this meeting: you are an asset to this organization in so many ways, especially in your ability to work under pressure, your willingness to take on additional tasks to help others meet their deadlines, and the accuracy of your work."

But everyone deserves recognition for whatever it is that they do well. As stated earlier, if there is absolutely nothing you can find to praise, then one has to wonder why the employee is still with the organization. Here is something you can say to an employee with numerous performance issues, but still does some things well: "Justin, despite the areas in which you need to improve, you continue to demonstrate an in-depth knowledge of the technical aspect of your job and that's impressive."

6. *Did I deliver criticism constructively?* Delivering criticism can be less stressful if you strive to be straightforward, are specific, provide a balanced picture, and are encouraging. Here is an example of criticism that is not constructive:

- "Tom, we've talked about your failure to focus on details a dozen times. You're just not getting it. I'm worried that the only way I'm going to get through to you is to write you up as part of our formal disciplinary process. Then maybe you'll understand how serious this is!"

Here is a more productive approach to constructive criticism:

- "Tom, in summary, we've talked about your need to better focus on details. You've identified some steps you feel will help you achieve this goal and I support them. Your work in many other areas is commendable; I'm confident that you'll succeed in elevating the level of your attention to detail if you adhere to the plan you've mapped out."

7. *Did I encourage the employee to make comments or ask questions?* Performance appraisal meetings consist of two-way communication. Earlier, we discussed the approximate ratio of talking and listening, with managers talking about twenty-five percent of the time. Remind yourself of this figure throughout the meeting and at the end ask yourself how successful you were in affording the employee most of the time commenting or asking questions. Just before ending, say, "Mandy, before concluding our meeting, do you have any additional comments or questions?"

8. *Did I reiterate my availability for help and support?* Remember that one of your primary responsibilities as a manager is that of a coach, whereby you are available to regularly offer assistance, support, praise, and constructive criticism (see Chapter 2). Reiterating this availability to the employee before ending the appraisal meeting can help to enhance employer-employee relations.

Becoming comfortable with conducting face-to-face perform-ance appraisal meetings begins with successfully applying effective interviewing skills. This includes setting the stage and differentiating among five recommended types of questions: competency-based, open-ended, hypothetical, probing, and close-ended. Each serves a distinct purpose and contributes toward making the performance appraisal meeting maximally productive. Additional interviewing skills include balancing talking with listening and practicing positive body language.

The appraisal meeting should focus on four key areas: past performance, previously set performance objectives, new performance objectives, and a career development plan for the employee. Throughout the process, the manager's role should be that of a facilitator.

Even when they have meticulously prepared a written review including ratings that are backed by specific examples, managers can be influenced by factors during the face-to-face meeting to the extent that they may be inclined to change their original evaluations. Pitfalls include allowing a recent accomplishment to overshadow an otherwise extensive pattern of poor performance, measuring an employee's performance against that of other employees rather than the responsibilities and requirements of the job, and excusing shortcomings in the employee that are similar to those of the manager. Once made aware of some of these pitfalls, however, managers are less likely to be influenced to change their original assessment.

No one will dispute that it is hard to tell an employee that his or her performance is unsatisfactory. But poor performers rarely improve without honest input by their managers.

Managers are advised to have a checklist identifying what needs to be covered in the appraisal meeting before concluding. Questions managers should ask of themselves include: Did I summarize past performance? Did we work together to set new performance objectives? Did I reinforce praise and end on a positive note? Did I deliver criticism constructively? And did I reiterate my availability for help and support?

Review Questions

1. Part of the performance appraisal meeting should focus on setting new performance objectives. These should be predicated on:
   (a) learning from one's mistakes.
   (b) the overall rating the employee receives.
   (c) how much money there is in the department's training budget.
   (d) how successful the employee has been in accomplishing past performance objectives.

   1. (d)

2. Having a checklist identifying what needs to be covered can help managers successfully conclude an appraisal meeting. One item on this list concerns the manager's offer of help and support. This serves as a reminder that one of a manager's primary responsibilities is that of a:
   (a) confidant.
   (b) counselor.
   (c) therapist.
   (d) coach.

   2. (d)

3. The number one way to effectively conduct negative appraisal meetings is for the manager to:
   (a) have an attorney present.
   (b) be honest.
   (c) wait till the date of the meeting to spring the news that the employee's performance is sub-par so he or she cannot mount a defense.
   (d) suggest that all is well, hoping that the employee will either improve or terminate.

   3. (b)

4. There are a number of appraisal pitfalls managers need to be wary of especially when conducting the face-to-face meeting. Perhaps the most influential factor of all is:
   (a) the employee's past performance.
   (b) the employee's attitude.
   (c) future goals of the employee.
   (d) the employee's personality.

   4. (a)

Do you have questions? Comments? Need clarification?
Call Educational Services at 1-800-225-3215, ext. 600,
or email at ed_svcs@amanet.org.

5. There are five recommended types of questions to ask during   5. (c)
the performance appraisal meeting. The type that focuses
on relating specific past job performance to probable future
on-the-job behavior is called a(n):
(a) probing question.
(b) open-ended question.
(c) competency-based question.
(d) hypothetical question.

7

Special Topics in Performance Appraisal

Learning Objectives

By the end of this chapter, you should be able to:

- Articulate what is needed to create and maintain a motivating atmosphere.
- Identify what workers really want.
- Differentiate between various mentoring relationships.
- Explain the value of managerial feedback.
- Identify the unique requirements for evaluating remote employees.
- Evaluate the merits of Web-based performance appraisals.

In this chapter we will examine several special topics in performance appraisal that fall outside the process we have just examined. Exploring these topics will help you gain insight into what motivates employees, the role of critical workplace relationships, the importance of feedback for managers, and two emerging topics in performance appraisal.

The following is a professional snapshot of Greg, a division manager in a mid-sized financial services company with a high degree of commitment to excellent performance appraisal practices. Let's see how this commitment translates into action.

As the manager of a division in a mid-sized financial services company, Greg is personally responsible for the work of six employees, one of whom works approximately seventy-five percent of the time from her home. He works hard at developing a good rapport with each, learning as much as he can about their respective interests and abilities as they relate to their current jobs and future aspirations.

Greg is especially proud of his approach to the company's performance appraisal process. He focuses year-round on his duties as a coach and counselor, maintaining an open, two-way communication. Greg diligently establishes and adheres to standards of performance, carefully prepares for appraisal meetings, gathers supporting information for ratings on the written review, and practices effective interviewing skills during the face-to-face meeting. With regard to the latter, Greg always feels gratified as an employee leaves his office, knowing that he is done the best he can to make the person feel good about himself or herself, even when it means delivering a less than flattering review.

Greg is also committed to meeting with employees according to the timeline jointly established to discuss progress made toward, or problems relating to, newly established performance objectives. This includes reviewing resources available and utilized; reiterating his availability for help and support; applauding employee accomplishments to date; amending the action plan, if needed; summarizing what remains to be accomplished; and confirming the next meeting date.

In addition, Greg works with employees toward helping them achieve their career goals. This occasionally means revising their Employee Career Development Plan, but these revisions are always made together with the employee, reflecting their wishes and relating them as much as possible to organizational goals.

Unquestionably, Greg views the performance appraisal as an integral part of effective employer-employee relations. More specifically, he understands that the performance appraisal process cannot effectively stand on its own, and that it represents neither the beginning nor the end of anything. To function effectively, the performance appraisal process requires support from senior management, human resources, managers, and employees.

While he cannot ensure this degree of support on his own, Greg knows there are factors beyond the performance appraisal that he can control: that is, things that will contribute to enhancing effective relations with his employees. In addition to all the steps identified above, Greg works toward creating and maintaining a motivating atmosphere, recognizing what workers really want, offering mentoring relationships toward further developing employee skills and interests, and ensuring his own professional development by accepting feedback from others.

In addition, Greg acknowledges the unique qualities associated with remote employment and practices, and respects the importance of maintaining the same level of effective employer-employee relations with the employee who works from her home as he does with on-site employees. Greg also knows that, increasingly, individuals at all levels favor electronic methods for accomplishing tasks. He is not sure if performance appraisals should go the way of the Internet, but he is interested in exploring the feasibility of Web-based performance appraisals.

Greg's attitudes and actions in turn inspire trust, loyalty, and a desire for success in his team. While life in Greg's division is not perfect, everyone stands to benefit from the group's commitment to open communication, honesty, and mutual respect.

CREATING AND MAINTAINING A MOTIVATING ATMOSPHERE

Much of a manager's effectiveness depends on his or her willingness and ability to understand what motivates an employee's behavior at any given time. The most effective managers continually ask themselves key questions:

- Is what currently motivates my employees the same as what motivated them at the time of hire?
- Is it likely that what motivates them now is what will continue to motivate them in the future?
- Is there anything that I, personally, can do to motivate my workers?
- Are there common denominators that motivate everyone?
- Are there theories or techniques that are applicable to everyone, regardless of what they are personally motivated by?

Inquisitive mangers learn that, as circumstances in a person's life change, so does what motivates them. Further, motivation is self-generated: their jobs as managers are to tap into what motivates employees and create a motivating environment. That said, there are factors that most workers are responsive too, and certain motivational theories address those factors.

Employee Motivation: An Overview

Every organization needs motivated employees in that they are what enable organizations survive, compete, and grow. By definition, workplace motivation is the inner voice that drives individuals to accomplish personal and organizational goals. It is fueled by achievement, development, and recognition. These will come naturally to employees whose managers fulfill their three primary roles:

- Helping employees make the best use of their own strengths and abilities.
- Recognizing employees for who they are.
- Helping employees find their own way.

A manager's secondary role is multi-tiered: that is, to encourage, support, inspire, link rewards with performance, and properly match employees with jobs.

A manager's ultimate goal with regard to employee motivation is to develop a virtually self-managing team. The true challenge for a manager comes with understanding that what motivates an individual changes constantly. For example, research shows that as an employee's income increases, money becomes less of a motivator. Also, as an employee grows older, interesting work becomes more of a motivator.

Unfortunately, many managers fail to understand what truly motivates their workers. They make the all too common mistake of implementing a "push or pull" strategy: "push" via threats, fear, or micromanaging of work; "pull" via the unrealistic promise of large bonuses, grandiose gifts, and other perks.

Motivational Theories

A handful of motivational theories developed in the mid- to late twentieth century laid the groundwork for our understanding of motivation in the workplace. Indeed, some of the more recent motivational theories are typically "variations on a theme" and are still awaiting acceptance on par with that of earlier theories. The theories highlighted here, some of which date back to the 1960s, are considered classics by many experts, and are as valid today as they were when first introduced. Here is a brief look at seven of them (Exhibit 7–1).

Theory X

Followers of Theory X believe that people inherently dislike work, are naturally lazy, and must be coerced or have their work controlled. They also maintain that people prefer to be directed over initiating work on their own. It is commonly believed that Theory X work environments are unhealthy for managers and employees alike: Managers cannot foster a creative work environment and employees are not free to pursue areas of interest.

Theory X is included among the select list of motivational theories to illustrate how a prevailing motivational philosophy can be counterproductive. Organizations that practice Theory X (and there are, unfortunately, many) produce a workforce that often feels disconnected from the big picture and lacks a sense of commitment or loyalty.

Theory Y

Proponents of Theory Y view work as being as natural as play. They believe people will exercise self-direction and self-control, as well as seek responsibility, in order to achieve their objectives. Theory Y work environments are considered highly conducive to employee growth and development. Douglas McGregor, of the Sloan School of Management at MIT, first described Theory X and Theory Y companies.

Theory Z

Supporters of Theory Z, developed by William Ouchi, maintain that input from workers at all levels is the key to increased productivity. It is based on a style of management with roots in strong company philosophy, long-range staff development, and consensus decision-making. Ouchi's theory came from observation of typical American companies (type A) and typical Japanese companies (type J). Ouchi believed that a blend of the best features of types A and J was best, including long-term employment, collective decision making, rapid evaluation and promotion, and a participative spirit.

 **xhibit 7–1**
Motivational Theories

Theory X:

- People inherently dislike work.
- Employees must be coerced into working.
- People prefer to be directed.

Theory Y:

- Work is as natural as play.
- Employees naturally exercise self-direction and self-control.
- Workers want to seek responsibility in order to achieve their objectives.

Theory Z:

- Input from workers at all levels is the key to increased productivity.
- Long-range staff development.
- Consensus decision-making.

Hierarchy of Needs Theory:

- Individuals have a natural, innate drive to achieve a state of self-actualization.
- There are five levels of needs, in the form of a triangle starting from the bottom with: physiological, safety, social, esteem needs.
- Self-actualization forms the pinnacle of the triangle.

Hygiene Theory:

- Satisfying "hygiene" factors, such as working conditions, salary, and security, allows us to pursue higher levels of motivation.
- Once hygiene needs are met people can be motivated by what they do on the job, such as achievement, recognition, and advancement.
- For maximum success, both hygiene and motivational factors must be satisfied.

Theory of Acquired Needs:

- Achievement
- Affiliation
- Power

Goal-Setting Theory:

- Challenging goals increases performance.
- Employees who accept difficult goals are more likely to succeed.
- People try harder and work smarter when striving to achieve challenging goals.

Hierarchy of Needs Theory
The hierarchy of needs theory, developed by Abraham Maslow, suggests that individuals have a natural, innate drive to achieve a state of healthfulness, or

self-actualization. Individuals have both biological and psychological needs that must be fulfilled so that they may be free enough to acknowledge their desire for the higher levels of realization. The hierarchy is commonly depicted in the mode of a triangle, with five levels of needs represented. Physiological needs serve as the foundation: these basic needs must be satisfied in order for individuals to aspire to the next level, which is safety. Once that need is satisfied, they can move on to meet their social needs, followed by need for esteem. Self-actualization forms the pinnacle of the triangle: the fifth level representing the ultimate state of achievement.

Hygiene Theory

According to this theory, developed by Frederick Herzberg and also known as the Two-Factor Theory, satisfying certain "hygiene" factors is essential to our well-being; without satisfying these factors, we experience dissatisfaction. Hygiene factors include: organizational policies and administration, the kind of supervision people receive, working conditions, interpersonal relations, salary, status, and security.

Proponents of this theory believe key hygiene factors meet a person's basic needs and provide individuals with an identity. The theory goes on to suggest that once hygiene needs are met, people can respond to another set of factors—"motivating" factors, which are tied to what and how they perform at work. Motivating factors include: achievement, recognition, growth or advancement, and a personal interest in one's work. For maximum success, both hygiene and motivational factors must be satisfied.

Theory of Acquired Needs

The theory of acquired needs, developed by David McClelland, identifies three key elements that individuals require in order to be motivated. They are: the need for achievement, the need for affiliation, and the need for power. A person's motivation and effectiveness in certain job functions are influenced by these three needs. Additional information about this theory appears later in the chapter.

Goal-Setting Theory

Followers of the Goal-Setting Theory believe that challenging goals increase performance. By accepting especially difficult goals, employees are more likely to perform at an optimum level than if given less complex goals. Employees who are encouraged to stretch toward achieving challenging goals will try harder and work smarter.

Motivational Theories in Relation to Employee Performance

Regardless of which motivational theories you support, it is irrefutable that people with varying needs are motivated differently. By example, let's use McClelland's Theory of Acquired Needs. As stated above, according to this theory (also known as the Three-Need Theory or the Learned Needs Theory), a person's motivation and effectiveness are influenced by three needs: achievement, affiliation, or power.

People with a high need for achievement seek to excel, and thus tend to avoid both low-risk and high-risk situations. They prefer work that has a moderate probability of success, and enjoy ongoing feedback in order to monitor and validate the progress of their achievements. They prefer either to work alone or with other high achievers.

Those with a high need for affiliation seek harmonious relationships with other people and want to feel accepted. They tend to conform to the norms of their work group, and prefer work that provides significant personal interaction.

A person's need for power can be one of two types: personal and social. Those who need personal power want to direct others; this need often is perceived as undesirable. Persons who seek social power enjoy organizing the efforts of others to further the goals of the organization.

Based on this motivational model, those employees demonstrating a high need for achievement should be given challenging projects with reachable goals, and should be provided with frequent feedback. Employees with a high affiliation need perform best in a cooperative environment. They tend to perform well in customer service and client interaction situations. By contrast, employees demonstrating a high need for power should be given the opportunity to manage others, assuming they have the necessary leadership skills to do so.

Managers who are closely attuned to the needs of their employees—that is, what motivates them—are likely to develop maximally effective employer-employee relations. This, in turn, will inevitably lend itself to a more productive exchange as well as the setting of more realistic performance objectives and career development plans during the employee's performance appraisal.

WHAT WORKERS REALLY WANT

For too long, employers have assumed that they know what workers want. Not surprisingly, many managers report that, in addition to workplaces that are safe and fair—that is, protected from health hazards and free from discrimination—high salaries, job security, and promotional opportunities are of primary importance to employees. Moreover, managers tend to assume that everyone in similar job classifications place the same degree of emphasis on the same work factors.

It is not that workers do not want economic security and a work environment free of unsafe and unfair employment practices; rather, they assume these basic tenets prevail. After all, with Occupational Health and Safety Administration (OSHA) regulations and multiple pieces of employment legislation banning workplace discrimination, why shouldn't employees assume they have the right to work in a safe, prejudice-free environment?

If they bothered to ask, employers might be surprised to learn what today's employees really want. Numerous surveys and studies reveal that what many employees seek is a feeling that they are making a positive impact in their jobs. Employees need to believe that the work they perform matters:

 **Think About It...**

Of the motivational theories cited, which do you think prevails in your organization?

_____ Theory X

_____ Theory Y

_____ Theory Z

_____ Hierarchy of Needs Theory

_____ Hygiene Theory

_____ Acquired Needs Theory

_____ Goal-Setting Theory

Of the theories that you checked off, which do you think is most effective in terms of positively impacting performance appraisals and ensuring a productive relationship between managers and employees? Support your answer.

Theory X

_____

_____

Theory Y

_____

_____

Theory Z

_____

_____

Hierarchy of Needs Theory

_____

_____

Hygiene Theory

_____

_____

Acquired Needs Theory

_____

_____

Goal-Setting Theory

_____

_____

_____

not necessarily in a grand way, but to someone, somewhere, somehow—they need to be told that their work is having a positive effect. The impact of their work can be communicated in any one of a number of ways, but the preferred method, according to employees, is via a word of personal thanks from their managers. When they do an especially good job, employees indicate that a word of thanks in the form of public praise goes a long way. This last statement is not surprising, given the long-standing piece of advice for managers to praise in public and criticize in private. Other employees report that they like having verbal praise solidified in the form of a written document in their HR files.

A Saratoga Institute survey of more than one thousand U.S. workers asked employees to identify factors that attracted them to organizations. The top three responses were: (1) performance evaluations based on a worker's ability to develop improved methods of doing things, (2) goals mutually developed by supervisors and the employee, and (3) job success based on the employee's responsibilities and accomplishments.

Additional factors that reportedly appeal to employees include:

- Personal attention
- Open communication between workers and managers
- Opportunities to gain new skills
- Opportunities for career advancement
- Challenges provided by their managers
- Working for a company that is committed to developing its workforce
- Respect on the part of a manager for his or her employees' lifestyle
- Working in a pleasant atmosphere
- Work that is fun, interesting, and exciting
- Self-fulfillment
- Being taken seriously
- Being treated with respect

Executives, too, have reported on factors that strongly influence their desire to work for one company over another. They cite an organization's values and culture as receiving high marks. Other factors that attract them include working for a well-managed company, the opportunity for career advancement, workplace challenges, the chance to work with many talented people, working for a company that is devoted to developing its workforce, and respect on the part of the employer for its employees' lifestyle. Money, while obviously appearing somewhere on everyone's list, rarely ranks high in importance. Having a fulfilling job is consistently considered more important.

When employees feel valued and believe management is responsive to their needs, they are likely to work harder at performing their duties and responsibilities at a maximally effective level. This often translates into higher ratings on performance appraisals. Employees are also likely to strive to better accomplish previously set performance objectives, and be better focused with regard to new performance objectives.

 **Think About It...**

If you were to poll workers in your organization, what three factors do you think they would say are of utmost importance to them?

1. _____

2. _____

3. _____

MENTORING

Mentoring may be defined as a developmental, helping relationship whereby one person invests time, ability, and effort toward enhancing another person's growth, knowledge, and skills in preparation for greater productivity or future achievement. Mentoring relationships may be situational, informal, or formal. Situational relationships are short, isolated incidences involving a casual transfer of information or ideas from one person to another. Informal mentoring involves personal relationships in which one person voluntarily shares expertise or knowledge with another. Formal mentoring programs are structured, are sanctioned by the organization, and focus on helping one or more individuals achieve specific goals. Accordingly, effective mentoring programs may be one-on-one, group, or team-to-team endeavors.

Mentoring can help employees achieve new performance objectives and further their career development plans. Tangentially, mentoring also enhances employee contributions to company productivity.

Here is what some individuals who have been mentored have said about their mentoring program experiences:

- "I'm contributing much more to our work team effort than I was just six months ago. I've been able to turn my whole attitude around. The mentoring experience has changed my life for the better."

- "I never dreamed that a highly successful executive could care so much about what would happen to me. I hope I can repay him by making good use of all those special insights he provided."

Now read what some mentors have reported:

- "When I help the person I am mentoring achieve something special and important to them, I feel I've made a powerful investment in our organization's most valuable asset—its people."

- "The very personal one-on-one investment in another person helped me to see each one as an individual and then our team as a synergy of harmonies, and as cooperative, unique individuals."

These representative comments illustrate how mentoring is a symbiotic relationship; that is, both mentors and those they mentor benefit.

Mentoring Programs

Mentoring programs can be one-on-one, group, or team-to-team. Personalized one-on-one mentoring has the greatest potential for trust and sharing, but it is not as practical as group or team mentoring. Having one executive mentor a group of four to six employees is by far more cost effective. In addition, participants can learn from their peers as well as from their mentor and having senior teams mentor junior teams exposes those they mentor to more than one set of skills and experiences.

The training of mentees is considered critical to the success of a mentoring program. Mentee training incorporates career assessment to identify goals, as well as guidance on what they can realistically expect as a result of the program. Mentor training entails conveying what their role consists of, the amount of time and energy required, and the importance of confidentiality.

Candidates for mentoring roles are selected on the basis of their skills, knowledge, availability, accessibility, interests, and rapport with potential mentees. Pairing up mentees with mentors may be accomplished in several different ways. Typically, matching assignments are made on the basis of defined needs of the mentees and the interests of the mentors. Sometimes, mentors and mentees are given several choices from which to choose.

Exactly how mentors and mentees communicate, and for how long, varies considerably depending on the established objectives and learning styles of the mentees. Generally, mentoring programs last about a year, but informal relationships may continue long after. Mentors and mentees usually meet every two weeks or so. If face-to-face meetings are impractical on a scheduled basis, they may regularly communicate by telephone, fax, or e-mail, bi-weekly or monthly, and then meet when feasible. Meetings usually last about two hours. In addition, any time a mentor comes across an article or hears of something relevant to the mentee's goals, he or she can convey it immediately, instead of waiting for a formal meeting.

Mentors are encouraged to familiarize themselves with the approach to learning preferred by their mentees. Some need to follow examples, some need to talk, and others need to experiment with different methods of accomplishing tasks. Regardless of the preferred methodology, mentees need to discover their own path to becoming effective. And mentors need to practice active listening, offer information and ideas, and provide frequent feedback.

Mentoring Programs in Relation to Performance Appraisals

By virtue of its very definition, mentoring ties in directly with performance appraisals: ". . . a developmental, helping relationship whereby one person invests time, ability, and effort in enhancing another person's growth, knowledge, and skills in preparation for greater productivity or future achievement." Poor performers can benefit from structured, formal, one-on-one mentoring programs while marginal employees needing an extra boost will do well in situational relationships. Exceptional employees seeking greater challenge and enhanced growth opportunities can develop through informal mentoring whereby one person voluntarily shares his or her expertise or knowledge. In truth, mentoring can help employees at every performance level achieve their greatest potential.

✎ Exercise: Types of Mentoring

Consider this scenario: You have an employee who does extremely well in her current job, but has expressed an interest in applying her skills to other segments of the organization. After some thought, you decide to recommend mentoring.

How would you go about determining whether she would benefit most from one-on-one, group, or team-to-team mentoring? Be specific.

_____

_____

_____

_____

HINTS, SUGGESTIONS, AND SOME ANSWERS

Factor in clarification of the employee's objectives and learning style (Does she need to talk? Follow examples? Experiment with different methods of accomplishing tasks?) Also, identify her preferred style of work (Does she work well as a member of a team or does she function more effectively on her own?) If the employee requires a good deal of attention, one-on-one mentoring will be effective; if she is responsive to learning from her peers, group mentoring may prove most beneficial; and if she currently functions as part of a team, the members of whom could all benefit from mentoring, then team mentoring may be the most desirable choice.

MANAGERIAL FEEDBACK

Jake is a manager in charge of his company's business products and services department. He has conducted approximately twenty performance appraisals over the past three years, and feels good about his success rate. When I asked him to define success, he replied, "I consider the performance appraisal to be successful when the employee and I agree on the ratings." That sounded reasonable, but incomplete, so I persisted: "Do you ask the employee to do a self-appraisal?" Jake replied affirmatively. "How about gathering input from peers, customers, and the like?" I asked. Jake again nodded in agreement.

I smiled as I prepared to ask the next question, anticipating that Jake would be startled by it: "When it's time to conduct an employee's appraisal, do you ask anyone to give you feedback on how you're doing as a manager?" Predictably, Jake stared for a moment before replying, "You're kidding, right?" "No, Jake, I'm not. Wouldn't it be helpful to receive input from others concerning how you're perceived when it comes to certain employer-employee relations matters? That way you can collate the information and apply it the next time you conduct a performance appraisal." What's one got to do with the other?" asked Jake.

"Let me answer with an example," I replied. "Imagine managerial feedback reveals that you're viewed as being fair and equitable in your treatment of staff. You prepare a review of an employee whom you feel needs to work on improving the quality of her work. Because of how you're perceived, it's more likely that she's going to receive your criticism with an open mind. If, on the other hand, you're perceived as showing favoritism and she's not one of your alleged favorites, she may not be as inclined to respond to what you have to say."

Before Jake could comment the telephone rang. It appeared that he was going to be on the telephone for some time, so I left. Jake never called me to continue our discussion.

The primary objective of managerial feedback—defined as the process whereby colleagues, customers, or anyone else with whom a manager has regular dealings offer feedback on his or her performance—is to maximize a manager's ability to fairly and accurately appraise workers. This process reinforces the appraising manager's commitment to open, two-way communication and allows for greater communication between managers and their employees. The manager's direct reports—that is, those employees for whom the manager conducts reviews—are also sometimes part of this process.

Ideally, managerial feedback should occur a month or so prior to the time when a manager conducts his or her performance appraisals. This is most feasible in organizations where all reviews are conducted on or around the same date. For example, if employee reviews are due between May 1 and May 15, managerial reviews would be due by April 15. If, on the other hand, appraisals are performed according to an employee's anniversary date (date of hire or date he or she moved into a new position), managerial feedback is best provided biannually.

Receiving feedback on one's own performance as a manager can be insightful, if viewed in the proper light. It is interesting to observe how many managers expect employees to be responsive to constructive criticism, but who themselves become defensive when "areas requiring improvement" are cited.

It is important to distinguish between managerial feedback and a manager's formal performance appraisal. A manager's formal review is conducted the same as any other employee's performance appraisal. Feedback, on the other hand, tells managers how others perceive them with regard to certain aspects of employer-employee relations.

Exhibit 7–2 identifies some recommended managerial feedback categories.

 **Think About It...**

Does your organization currently offer remote employment as an option to traditional work arrangements? _____ yes _____ no

If you answered "yes," how responsive are managers to monitoring the performance of remote employees? _____ very responsive _____ somewhat responsive _____ resistant

If you answered "no," how responsive do you think managers would be to monitoring the performance of remote employees? _____ very responsive _____ somewhat responsive _____ resistant. Explain your answer: _____

PERFORMANCE APPRAISALS FOR REMOTE EMPLOYEES

Wendy woke up with a pounding headache. She looked at the clock and knew she had to start getting ready in order to arrive at work on time. As she struggled to her feet she glanced outside and saw that it was snowing heavily. She groaned, "I wish I could just work from home today."

Everyone has had days like this. We want the flexibility of getting our work done without going into the office every day. In addition to the obvious pluses from an employee's perspective, businesses also benefit from off-site, or remote, employment. They save on utilities, expand their recruiting base beyond the immediate geographic area, and utilize the services of individuals who cannot physically commute on a regular basis.

What Is Remote Employment?

Remote employment is a work arrangement whereby employees perform some of their duties and responsibilities at home, or at another off-site location instead of regularly commuting to an office or other specified workplace. Many remote employees spend from several days a week to several weeks or months a year working out of their homes or at satellite sites. Remote managers, who see these employees on anywhere from a frequent to an occasional basis, monitor work through a combination of traditional and electronic means.

Performance Monitoring

It is not unusual for managers to express concern over the lack of direct control of a remote employee's work. When you are accustomed to a work environment where managers perform their jobs observing and interacting with employees directly, it can be challenging to adjust to the world of virtual management.

Here are some of the questions managers commonly ask about the performance of remote employees:

 **xhibit 7–2**

Managerial Feedback

Instructions: Please answer the questions below as they relate to (name). Provide specific examples to support each response. Skip any questions for which you lack sufficient first-hand knowledge. Your answers will be kept anonymous, unless you indicate otherwise.

What would you identify as (name's) greatest strengths? Provide as many strengths as you wish, with support for each response.

_____

_____

_____

On a scale of 1–10, with 1 representing the least ideal, and 10 representing the most ideal, how successful is (name) in applying these strengths to employer-employee relations?

_____

_____

What would you identify as areas in which (name) needs improvement? Provide as many areas as you wish, with support for each response.

_____

_____

_____

Do any of these areas requiring improvement impede effective employer-employee relations? _____ yes _____ no. Please explain:

_____

_____

Does (name) encourage employees to ask questions or seek clarification regarding their work assignments? _____ yes _____ no. Please explain:

_____

_____

Is (name) available and supportive in instances during which employees have had an especially difficult assignment or challenging deadline to meet? _____ yes _____ no. Please explain:

_____

_____

Exhibit continued on next page

Exhibit 7–2   continued from previous page

Would you describe (name) as a good listener? _____ yes _____ no. Please explain:

_____

_____

What is your description of the ideal manager?

_____

_____

On a scale of 1–10, with 1 representing the furthest from ideal and 10 representing the most ideal, how would you rate (name) as a manager? _____ Please explain:

_____

_____

_____

- How can I determine if there is a situation that calls for coaching?
- How can I counsel an employee about violating a work-related policy before it spirals out of control, when I am not there to ensure compliance?
- How can I measure a remote employee's performance against the duties and responsibilities identified in his job description when I cannot check on his or her work first-hand?
- How can I determine how well an employee is able to cope with pressure and effectively balance multiple projects simultaneously when I am not around to see?
- Can I really get to know an employee with whom I rarely interact?

These concerns are all valid; they are also manageable. Addressing them begins with effective communication.

The importance of consistent and purposeful communication with remote employees cannot be overemphasized. While many of the standard employer-employee communication techniques are applicable, the unique nature of remote employment calls for special consideration. Managers and their remote employees need to find the right balance between keeping each other updated and informed, without imposing a communication burden.

The expression, "out of sight, out of mind," has particular meaning when applied to remote employees. Managers who are geographically distanced from their workers may get so caught up in their own tasks that they fail to give the necessary attention to the efforts of this group of employees. That is why it is so important to maintain a practice of ongoing communication: that is, staying in touch regularly in a variety of ways.

Communication via Telephone

Managers should maintain regular voice contact with remote employees. The frequency of voice contact will depend largely on the nature of the job,

Think About It...

As a manager, using a scale of 1–10 with 10 signifying "maximally responsive," and 1 signifying "minimally responsive," how are you likely to respond overall to feedback from:

_____ your colleagues?

_____ customers, clients, vendors?

_____ direct reports?

How are you likely to respond in particular to feedback that differs considerably from how you view yourself?

_____

_____

_____

What are the chances that you would make changes in your managerial style or behavior based on managerial feedback if there is a consensus that differs from how you view yourself? _____ very likely _____ somewhat likely _____ not very likely _____ highly unlikely

Would managerial feedback influence how you conduct performance appraisals?

_____ probably _____ possibly _____ it's unlikely _____ absolutely not

how comfortable the employee is in working independently, how much confidence the manager has in the remote employee's ability and willingness to function effectively off-site, and the overall relationship between manager and employee. For some remote workers, this will mean daily telephone contact; for others, it may necessitate talking no more than once a week, or perhaps even less frequently.

Even with those employees who are extremely capable of working independently and report to highly confident managers, some regular telephone contact should feature in the reporting relationship. E-mails are great, but they cannot convey tone of voice, inflection, pauses in speech, or emphasis (forget about using caps—THEY ALWAYS MAKE IT APPEAR THAT THE PERSON IS YELLING.). These telephone calls, lasting from a few minutes to a half-hour or so, can include a discussion of problems, status reports, areas of accomplishment, questions, suggestions, and any other topic deemed appropriate.

These are check-in and catch-up telephone calls. Preferably, a certain time during each workday should be designated "talk time," when both manager and employee are likely to be available: this should not turn into a game of "telephone tag." Note the reference to telephone calls during the workday: talking with remote employees is part of a manager's job; as such, it should not spill over into nonworking hours for either party.

Electronic Communication

Technology makes remote working relationships possible. Electronic communication in the form of e-mail and instant messaging (IM), as well as Web meetings, virtual bulletin boards, and videoconferencing all facilitate virtual interactions, allowing for exchanges that are as close to "real" as possible when people are geographically remote.

While it is true that electronic communication cannot substitute for face-to-face meetings or convey a person's tone of voice or vocal inflection, it does provide an instantaneous connection between managers and remote employees that can be gratifying and productive.

E-mails and IMs are clearly the electronic formats of choice. They are cheap, easy to compose, and can be transmitted quickly. Significantly, differences in location and time zones become irrelevant. This makes it extremely easy for managers to monitor the performance of remote employees.

While there is no limit to the possible topics and content areas for e-mail messages, they fall into three basic communication categories:

- *Providing information:* Here is an e-mail sent by a manager to one of her remote employees working on a long-term project: "I'm including some additional resources you may find helpful in working on the Universal Synergy project. I've also attached a couple of related articles; hope you find that it provides interesting reading and some useful information."
- *Requesting information:* The manager's e-mail could continue with, "Where did you put Universal's most recent status report?"
- *Requesting action:* "Please send me a chronological list of everything you've discussed in meetings or otherwise covered with respect to Universal. I'll also need the corresponding spreadsheet. IM me today by 5:00PM my time to verify. Thanks!"

In addition to providing and requesting information and requesting action, e-mails enable managers to share news from the home office, send photographs of company events, mail eCards with birthday greetings or messages of congratulations on a job well done, or send a simple 'Hi, how's it going?'

Face-to-Face Communication

As previously stated, no electronic communication tool or technique can substitute for the visual cues provided through body language or an auditory exchange between a manager and his or her direct reports. This includes both Web meetings and videoconferencing. Logistics will largely dictate the frequency of meetings and most experts recommend a minimum of four face-to-face meetings a year. For internationally situated remote employees that might be adequate, whereas team members who are not so geographically distant can and should meet far more frequently, from once a month to once a week. These meetings let employees know that the work they perform is important to the organization. It also reaffirms the employer-employee relationship and provides valuable insight into an individual's performance.

Avoid the trap of assuming that top or average performers require less personal attention than marginal employees. All employees require a measure of praise and encouragement along with constructive feedback. Try to time your visits so that they coincide with celebratory events, such as the successful completion of a project or the opening of a new store. If you only appear when there are problems, employees will come to view you as the bearer of bad news.

Building a Relationship with Remote Employees

Communicating regularly by telephone and e-mail and in person allows managers to build relationships with their remote employees. In a typical workplace setting, managers and workers get to know one another through numerous informal encounters: a casual conversation in the parking lot or elevator, a few words exchanged at the coffee machine or water cooler, or an impromptu visit by one to the other's office. In and of themselves, none of these occurrences are significant; however, together they serve to form the foundation that ultimately becomes a relationship between employer and employee. Through each encounter, over a period of days, weeks, and months, managers and employees get to learn about each other.

Clearly, this "getting to know you" dance cannot be duplicated with remote employees but it can be modified and still have a positive impact. Consider the manager with a virtual water cooler. He invites his remote employees to spend time with him at his cooler, just "hanging out," talking about whatever happens to come up. These "meetings" are regular events, scheduled at times that are convenient for all concerned. While this is basically instant messaging, the fact that it is called a water cooler and emphasizes non-work topics makes it more employee-friendly. In essence, the manager is building a virtual workplace community that encourages everyone to get to know one another better, just as they might if working in the same office.

Building a relationship with remote employees is also more likely to occur if you stress the degree of trust you have in their ability to do their jobs in a timely fashion. This can be challenging, as many managers feel uneasy about their lack of control over employees' work. They cannot physically see them perform, overhear telephone conversations, ensure a full day's work, or even know if they are where they are supposed to be.

If you feel stressed about not being able to personally monitor employee performance, consider the words of advice offered by Loretta Castorini, a character from the film *Moonstruck*: "Snap out of it!" You should not be hovering over employees in the office, and the fact that you cannot hover over remote employees means that you are managing the way you should. Assign a task and leave the person alone to do his or her job. Be available for help (on- or off-site), but otherwise step aside to allow employees do their work.

Successful remote relationships are predicated upon managers having sufficient confidence in their own ability to manage and trust in the employees they have working for them—whether in the office or off-site. When employees feel that they are trusted, they are more likely to contribute at a high level. Reassure employees that you have confidence in their ability to perform their jobs and then let them demonstrate what they can do.

Performance Measurement

Managers of on-site employees tend to be process-focused. They measure and assess the effectiveness of a worker's performance based, in part, on the degree of effort expended, offering positive and corrective feedback in the form of coaching and counseling, as warranted. When it comes to remote employees, however, some managers find it difficult to advise, assess, and give feedback to employees who are not physically present. These managers need to shift their focus to results; that is, judge employees on output, not "face time." Stated another way, they should concentrate on measuring productivity, not activity. Their commitment should be to evaluate employees based on how well mutually agreed-on goals are achieved, as opposed to what they observe on a daily basis.

Measurement Criteria

Earlier in this chapter, you read some of the most commonly asked questions posed by managers about the performance of remote employees. Let's revisit these questions, and see what measurement criteria pertain:

Q: *How can I determine if there's a situation that calls for coaching?*
A: Managing off-site employees warrants an expansion of the 360-degree evaluation (see Chapter 3). Rather than relying on feedback from individuals with whom the remote employee has contact solely at the time of the formal appraisal, managers should regularly communicate with them to identify areas that might call for assistance, support, praise, and constructive criticism. Managers can also periodically solicit informal self-appraisals. In addition, daily telephone conversations and frequent e-mails are likely to reveal situations calling for coaching.

Q: *How can I counsel an employee about violating a work-related policy before it spirals out of control if I am not there to ensure compliance?*
A: If feedback from individuals with whom the remote employee has contact reveals performance concerns, managers must address them immediately. This should be accomplished face-to-face, with the manager traveling to meet the employee, not the other way around. As with coaching, the essence of counseling is the same with remote workers as it is for on-site employees; that is, following a sequence of predetermined steps, the goal of which is to rectify a work-related issue.

Q: *How can I measure a remote employee's performance against the duties and responsibilities identified in his job description when I cannot check on his work firsthand?*
A: Provide remote employees with copies of their job descriptions. At least quarterly, ask them to review the content and submit a report to you, identifying specific areas where they feel they excel and/or need improvement. Require supporting examples. In addition, if feasible, pose the question: "If I were to ask (name of someone familiar with the position) to measure your performance

against the duties and responsibilities identified in your job description, what would she say?"

Q: *How can I determine how well an employee is able to cope with pressure and effectively balance multiple projects simultaneously when I am not around to see?*

A: For each project, create a task list; then check off items as they are completed. Depending on the complexity of these tasks, managers can request progress reports at regular intervals identifying the following: overall and specific objectives, steps, timeline, individual components, resources available, resources used, projected time required for completion, and actual time required for completion.

Q: *Can I really get to know an employee with whom I rarely interact?*

A: Yes. Communicate often and through varied means, including frequent telephone calls and e-mails and regularly scheduled face-to-face meetings. Be patient; getting to know anyone takes time. Learning about a remote employee is really no different from becoming acquainted with the behaviors and work habits of an on-site worker.

✎ Exercise: Remote Employment

Consider this scenario: While Greg acknowledges the unique requirements of supervising remote employees and respects the importance of maintaining the same level of communication and supervision with his remote employee as he does with his on-site team, he is having trouble "letting go." Specifically, he cannot help but wonder if she is really working while at home.

Provide five suggestions that will help Greg feel less uneasy about remote employment:

1. _____
2. _____
3. _____
4. _____
5. _____

HINTS, SUGGESTIONS, AND SOME ANSWERS

- Maintain regular telephone contact on a daily or weekly basis.
- Generate frequent exchanges of e-mails and IMs.
- Meet face-to-face as frequently as logistically possible.
- Be mindful of areas that might call for coaching and counseling and address them the same as with on-site employees.
- Ask remote employees to review their job descriptions and periodically submit a report, identifying specific areas where they feel they excel and/or need improvement.

WEB-BASED PERFORMANCE APPRAISALS

With so many aspects of our lives being affected by the capabilities of electronic delivery, is it far-fetched to think of converting your organization's existing paper performance appraisal system into a Web-based system? Just as some organizations have converted to electronic employment applications, so too are companies beginning to turn to electronic means to help assess employee accomplishments.

Web-based performance appraisals are unique in that, unlike paper-based reviews, they rely on software that allows for the immediate access of all documents, journal entries, prior reviews, and records relevant to the appraisal process. Computer programs can provide lists of all employees, the status of each person's review, past objectives, relevant milestones, as well as suggested comments and phrases to avoid. In essence, Web-based performance appraisals are increasingly capable of providing every level of every step for every employee who is subject to the performance review process.

Are Web-based appraisals right for your organization? While the actual decision to convert to Web-based performance appraisals will likely be made by members of senior management and human resources, it will have a direct impact on manager-employee relations. Therefore, you should become informed and prepared.

Advantages of Web-Based Performance Appraisals

Supporters maintain that the primary advantage of a Web-based performance appraisal system is the ease with which it enables managers to comply with review-related responsibilities. An automated appraisal system can generate and retain a great deal of data, thereby reducing the extent to which managers must gather, organize, and sift through performance-related information. Other advantages include immediate access to performance information by others with a need to know, and reduced time spent drafting and reviewing written reviews. Ongoing updates of performance objectives and career development plans are also possible, as is aligning personal goals with organizational objectives.

Disadvantages of Web-Based Performance Appraisals

As with any new automated system, there are kinks in Web-based performance appraisal systems that can impair the timely delivery of reviews. Also, Web-based systems can be expensive to install and complex to learn. A significant amount of technical support may be required, and there are security concerns that must be addressed. There is also concern that, once automated, managers who barely spoke with their employees except for the occasion of the annual review, will have even less contact. Essentially, detractors view the process as dehumanizing what should be a person-to-person process.

Appraisal Software

There are a number of performance appraisal software products available for purchase. Essentially, while differences exist among specific offerings, they all basically provide the following:

- A variety of forms and templates for different job families and classifications
- Tips and suggestions concerning how to complete forms and conduct effective face-to-face meetings
- Advice to managers about providing specific examples to support ratings
- Built-in "employment law attorneys" that flag inappropriate and/or illegal terminology (such as "bad attitude") and any personal information
- A variety of terms and phrases to support numerical ratings

---

?   **Think About It...**

How responsive do you think the managers in your organization would be to Web-based performance appraisals? _____ extremely responsive _____ somewhat responsive _____ not at all responsive. Support your answer.

_____

_____

How responsive do you think the employees in your organization would be to Web-based performance appraisals? _____ extremely responsive _____ somewhat responsive _____ not at all responsive. Support your answer.

_____

_____

What do you perceive to be the greatest hurdle that would have to be overcome if your organization implemented Web-based performance appraisals?

_____

_____

Do you think it would be possible to have both Web-based performance appraisals and paper appraisals in your organization, giving managers the option of which one they wanted to use? _____ yes _____ no _____ maybe. Support your answer.

_____

_____

_____

_____

Performance appraisal software allows the user to access any one of a number of categories that could be part of a performance appraisal, such as "extent of knowledge." Based on the accompanying list of descriptive terms, you can select a rating. As soon as you make your selection, phrases relating to the category appear. You may then choose the one you feel most accurately describes the employee. The ability to insert the employee's name is available, thereby adding a degree of personalization.

Some of the phrases tend to be simplistic, such as "effective," or "tries hard, but doesn't always succeed." Others are somewhat convoluted: for example, "William does an excellent job when he decides he wants to apply himself, which is not always the case." Sometimes there are no phrases that accurately describe the employee being reviewed. When that happens, some programs allow managers to edit the language. However, given the aversion many managers have toward writing reviews, it is not uncommon for managers to simply accept what may be a less accurate phrase.

Much of a manager's effectiveness depends on his or her willingness and ability to understand what motivates an employee's behavior. The most effective managers will continually ask themselves key questions, such as "Is what currently motivates my employees the same as what motivated them at the time of hire?" and "Is it likely that what motivates them now will continue to motivate them in the future?"

Unfortunately, many managers fail to understand what truly motivates their workers, and so they turn to various motivational theories for guidance. Some of the theories that have proven their worth over time include: Theory Y, Theory Z, Hierarchy of Needs Theory, Hygiene Theory, Theory of Acquired Needs, and Goal-Setting Theory.

Regardless of which motivational theories you support, it is irrefutable that people with different needs are motivated differently. Managers who are closely attuned to the needs of their employees are likely to develop maximally effective employer-employee relations; this in turn, will lend itself to a more productive exchange during the employee's performance appraisal.

Employers have long assumed that they know what workers want, citing safety and fair employment practices high on the list. While these factors are important to workers to the point where they take them for granted, numerous studies and surveys reveal that employees really need to believe that the work they perform is meaningful. When they do an especially good job, employees indicate that a word of thanks in the form of public praise goes a long way. When employees feel valued and believe management is responsive to their needs, they are likely to perform their duties and responsibilities at a maximally effective level. Often this translates into higher ratings on performance appraisals. Employees are also more likely to strive toward better accomplishing previously set performance objectives, and be more focused with regard to new performance goals.

Mentoring may be defined as a developmental, helping relationship whereby one person invests time, ability, and effort in enhancing another person's growth, knowledge, and skills in preparation for greater productivity or future achievement. Mentoring can help employees achieve new performance objectives and further their career development plans. Mentoring programs can be one-on-one, group, or team-to-team. Mentoring can help employees at every performance level achieve their greatest potential.

The primary objective of managerial feedback is to maximize a manager's ability to fairly and accurately appraise workers. Asking colleagues, customers, or anyone else with whom a manager has regular dealings for feedback reinforces the appraising manager's commitment to open communication and allows for maximally effective employer-employee relations.

Remote employment is a work arrangement whereby employees perform some of their duties and responsibilities at home, or at some other off-site location instead of regularly commuting to an office or other specified workplace. It is not unusual for managers to express concern over the lack of direct control over a remote employee's work. The key to successfully managing the performance of remote employees is consistent and purpose-ful communication.

Just as some organizations have converted to electronic employment applications, so, too, are companies beginning to rely on their computers to assess employee accomplishments. Advantages include ease for managers to comply with review-related responsibilities; disadvantages include cost and complexity of use.

Review Questions

1. A manager's formal review is conducted the same as any other employee's performance appraisal. Feedback, on the other hand, tells managers:
   (a) what they are doing wrong.
   (b) how others perceive them with regard to certain aspects of employer-employee relations.
   (c) ways in which their employees want them to change.
   (d) how their superiors view their work.

   1. (b)

2. While one-on-one mentoring has the greatest potential for trust and sharing, it is not as practical as:
   (a) group or team mentoring.
   (b) training and development workshops.
   (c) hiring retirees.
   (d) fostering a Theory X work environment.

   2. (a)

3. A manager's ultimate goal with regard to employee motivation is to develop:
   (a) a workforce consisting of employees who are so well matched with their jobs that they are content to remain in them for a long time.
   (b) a workforce consisting of employees who understand that in order to be truly content they need to put their personal goals before those of the organization.
   (c) a virtually self-managing team.
   (d) a "push and pull" strategy that keeps employees on their toes.

   3. (c)

4. One key concern connected with Web-based performance appraisals is that:
   (a) they will become a technological nightmare.
   (b) managers who barely spoke with their employees except for the occasion of the annual review will now have even less contact with them.
   (c) they will not preclude managers from using inappropriate or illegal terminology.
   (d) everyone will end up with the same basic review.

   4. (b)

Do you have questions? Comments? Need clarification?
Call Educational Services at 1-800-225-3215, ext. 600,
or email at ed_svcs@amanet.org.

5. Successful remote relationships are predicated on: 5. (d)
- (a) the amount of direct control managers have over the work of remote employees.
- (b) how advanced the organization's electronic equipment is.
- (c) the percentage of time remote employees spend in the office.
- (d) managers having sufficient confidence in their own ability to manage and trust in the employees they have working for them—whether in the office or off-site.

Bibliography

Books

Arthur, Diane. *The Recruitment and Retention Handbook.* (New York: AMACOM, 2001).

Arthur, Diane. *Recruiting, Interviewing, Selecting and Orienting New Employees.* (4th Ed.) (New York: AMACOM, 2006).

Bascal, Robert. *Performance Management.* (New York: McGraw-Hill, 1999).

DelPo, Amy. *The Performance Appraisal Handbook, Legal & Practical Rules for Managers.* (Berkeley, CA: Nolo, 2005).

Falcone, Paul. *101 Sample Write-Ups for Documenting Employee Performance Problems.* (New York: AMACOM, 1999).

Grote, Dick. *The Complete Guide to Performance Appraisal.* (New York: AMACOM, 1996).

Grote, Dick. *The Performance Appraisal Question & Answer Book, A Survival Guide for Managers.* (New York: AMACOM, 2002).

Harvard Business Review on Appraising Employee Performance. (Boston: Harvard Business School Press, 2005).

Schwartz, Andrew E. *Performance Management.* (Hauppauge, NY: Barron's Educational Series, 1999).

Self-Study

Arthur, Diane. *Fundamentals of Human Resources Management.* (4th Ed.) (New York: American Management Association, 2004).

Magazines

HR *Magazine,* from the Society for Human Resource Management: 1800 Duke Street, Alexandria, VA 22314. Tel: 703/548-3440; fax: 703/836-0367; E-mail: *shrm@shrm.org.*

T+D, from the American Society for Training & Development: 1640 King Street, Box 1443, Alexandria, VA 22313. Fax: 703/683-9591; E-mail: *mailbox@astd.org.*

Workforce Management from Crain Communications, Inc.: 245 Fischer Avenue B-2, Costa Mesa, CA 92626. E-Mail: *raphaelt@workforce.com.*

Newsletters

HR Manager's Legal Reporter, Ransom & Benjamin Publishers LLC: 21 East Main Street, Mystic, CT 06355. Tel: 860/536-2000; Fax: 860-536-1545; E-mail: *rhpuborders@aol.com.*

Web Sites

www.astd.org

www.rhpubs.com

www.shrm.org/hrresources/articles

www.workforce.com

Post-Test

Performance Appraisals: Strategies for Success

Course Code 95083

INSTRUCTIONS: *Record your answers on one of the scannable forms enclosed. Please follow the directions on the form <u>carefully</u>. Be sure to keep a copy of the completed answer form for your records. <u>No photocopies will be graded.</u> When completed, mail your answer form to:*

Educational Services
American Management Association
P.O. Box 133
Florida, NY 10921

1. At the end of the appraisal meeting, the manager should work together with the employee in setting new goals. This process should include:
   (a) the promise of a raise if the employee meets his or her new goals.
   (b) a timeline to review progress and identify problems.
   (c) configured and prefigured tasks.
   (d) written progress reports.

Do you have questions? Comments? Need clarification?
Call Educational Services at 1-800-225-3215, ext. 600,
or email at ed_svcs@amanet.org.

2. The appraisal method that involves the greatest amount of input from numerous sources, and may be considered the one most likely to provide a well-rounded evaluation is called:
(a) a behaviorally anchored rating scale.
(b) a graphic rating scale
(c) management by objectives.
(d) a 360-degree evaluation.

3. Managers need to balance the amount of talking they do with listening. In reality, managers should devote no more than:
(a) twenty-five percent of the time talking.
(b) fifteen percent of the time talking.
(c) an equal amount of time talking and listening.
(d) the amount of time required by the employee—some employees are better listeners than talkers.

4. An important step in the preparation stage is for managers to anticipate possible employee reactions to their appraisals. One way of dealing with an overconfident employee is to:
(a) emphasize the areas in which they need to improve.
(b) provide them with additional, challenging responsibilities.
(c) ask them to present documentation as evidence of all their accomplishments.
(d) mirror their behavior.

5. An effective performance appraisal system requires the cooperation and input of human resources practitioners, managers, and employees in which everyone involved in the process is responsible for:
(a) ensuring consistency between comments, ratings, and any recommended action to be taken.
(b) completing a self-evaluation.
(c) applying applicable employment laws.
(d) looking for ways in which to enhance or improve the performance appraisal system.

6. Web-based performance appraisals are gaining acceptance in some organizations because they:
(a) are cost-effective.
(b) eliminate the need for managers to sit, face-to-face, with an employee and deal with possible adverse reactions.
(c) make it easier for managers to comply with review-related responsibilities.
(d) allow managers to give every employee the same basic review, thereby eliminating any possible charges of discrimination.

7. An important question managers should ask themselves during the preparation stage of conducting employee performance appraisals is:
   (a) Does the employee respect me and trust that I will give him or her a fair appraisal?
   (b) Have I objectively measured the employee's work record against the requirements of the job?
   (c) Do I have a right to appraise an employee performing a job that I, myself, have never held?
   (d) Would I be better off asking a professional to write the review? Then I can just refer to it during the face-to-face meeting.

8. The first of four key ways in which employees can benefit from and use performance appraisals that have nothing to do with money is:
   (a) the opportunity to receive a clearer understanding of what they are expected to do.
   (b) the opportunity to let human resources know what really goes on in their department.
   (c) nothing—this is a trick question; everything has to do with money.
   (d) the opportunity to justify an out-of-town conference to learn new skills.

9. Of the seven motivational theories described, the one that stands out as contrary to all the others is:
   (a) Theory Z.
   (b) the Hierarchy of Needs Theory.
   (c) the Theory of Acquired Needs.
   (d) Theory X.

10. You will discuss four main areas in a performance appraisal meeting: past performance, previously set performance objectives, new performance objectives, and:
   (a) the employee's career development plan.
   (b) the percentage raise being recommended.
   (c) how the employee plans to work on areas requiring improvement.
   (d) how the employee can benefit from the company's mentor program.

11. One of the best-known pieces of civil rights legislation and the most widely used, in that it protects several classes of people and pertains to so many employment situations, including performance appraisals, is the:
   (a) Civil Rights Act of 1991.
   (b) Civil Rights Act of 1964.
   (c) Immigration Reform and Control Act of 1986.
   (d) Equal Pay Act of 1963.

12. Many managers resist participating in the performance appraisal process because:
(a) they are not getting paid enough money to deal with the range of possible employee reactions to their reviews.
(b) they have never been taught how.
(c) employees should conduct self-appraisals.
(d) performance appraisals belong in the hands of human resources.

13. Of the five recommended interviewing questions, the type that allows for the evaluation of reasoning abilities, thought processes, attitudes, creativity, work style, and one's approach to different tasks is:
(a) probing.
(b) open-ended.
(c) hypothetical.
(d) competency-based.

14. The type of coaching that requires managers to be attentive and attuned to each employee's individual work habits, routines, and current assignments is called:
(a) spontaneous coaching.
(b) planned coaching.
(c) directive coaching.
(d) nondirective coaching.

15. Throughout the year, between formal performance appraisal reviews, managers are responsible for observing and noting:
(a) employee accomplishments and areas requiring improvement.
(b) documented evidence to support termination.
(c) initiative.
(d) how successful employees are at meeting performance objectives from the previous year.

16. As part of a progressive disciplinary procedure, following a second written warning for excessive absenteeism, an employee should be:
(a) terminated.
(b) suspended with or without pay.
(c) sent for counseling.
(d) issued a third written warning.

17. Managers are advised to begin planning the contents of a written performance appraisal approximately:
(a) one month prior to the due date.
(b) one week prior to the due date.
(c) two weeks prior to the due date.
(d) two months prior to the due date.

18. The primary distinction between coaching and counseling is that coaching involves day-to-day interaction between managers and employees in which managers regularly offer assistance, support, praise, and constructive criticism. Counseling, on the other hand, involves:
    (a) progressive discipline.
    (b) legal counsel.
    (c) the final stage before termination.
    (d) a structured interaction between managers and their employees; managers focus on particular work-related issues.

19. In order to be effective, a performance appraisal system should practical, workable, and viewed by all as:
    (a) a matter of law.
    (b) disposable; that is, replaced as soon as a new appraisal is written.
    (c) a helpful tool for achieving organizational goals.
    (d) nonnegotiable.

20. Managers commonly have an aversion to conducting negative appraisal meetings. They hope that the employee's work will improve on its own, or that:
    (a) the employee will take pity on them and shape up.
    (b) the employee will transfer or terminate.
    (c) the employee will seek counseling.
    (d) human resources will realize what is going on and step in to intervene.

21. When writing job descriptions, prior experience requirements should accurately and realistically reflect the level and nature of the position. An example of a tangible experience requirement is:
    (a) a pleasant personality.
    (b) a proven ability to successfully communicate with attendees of training programs.
    (c) a college degree.
    (d) a demonstrated ability to lift cartons weighing 20–40 lbs.

22. Mentoring relationships are determined on the basis of:
    (a) the defined needs of the mentees and the interests of the mentors.
    (b) the status of the mentor in the organization.
    (c) how much help the mentee requires.
    (d) a lottery.

23. Subjective language reflects one's personal opinion and may be subject to interpretation. An example is that:
    (a) Jill has the technical skills required of this job.
    (b) Jill has five years' previous experience performing similar tasks.
    (c) Jill has demonstrated her ability to do this job.
    (d) I think Jill has what it takes to do this job!

24. When evaluating the long-term effectiveness of communication skills, managers find measurable results are more likely to continue when they provide:
   (a) annual increases in pay.
   (b) constructive criticism and training.
   (c) ongoing feedback and encouragement.
   (d) promotional and transfer opportunities.

25. Managerial feedback can serve to:
   (a) identify areas requiring improvement.
   (b) maximize a manager's ability to fairly and accurately appraise workers.
   (c) reveal a side of a manager no one has ever seen before.
   (d) determine whether he or she has executive potential.

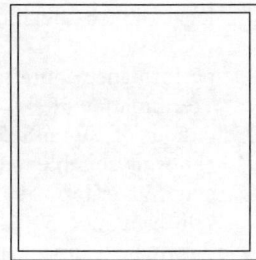

Index